HARD WORK:

THE GRETA VAN FLEET STORY

NY Times Best-seller
MARC SHAPIRO

For more information contact:
Riverdale Avenue Books
5676 Riverdale Avenue
Riverdale, NY 10471

www.riverdaleavebooks.com

Design by www.formatting4U.com
Cover by Scott Carpenter
Cover photo by Lori Perkins

Digital ISBN: 9781626015272

Print ISBN: 9781626015289

First Edition November, 2019
Second Edition, August, 2024

This Book is Dedicated to…

All those who count. My wife Nancy… Through thick and thin, love always. My daughter Rachael… A fighter who brings out the best in me. Lily… the perfect grandchild for the coming age. Brent… rock on. Brady… RIP. Lady… Welcome to our world. Max… Good dog. Lori Perkins… A pro's pro in so many ways. Riverdale Avenue Books… the publisher that keeps on giving. All the good books, music and art… the things that make life an endless series of happy surprises.

And finally to Greta Van Fleet, who are living proof that hard work is its own reward.

Table of Contents

Author's Notes
The Natural Order of Metal

Let's address the 800-pound gorilla in the room. I'll give you a hint. "Stairway To Heaven," "Whole Lotta Love," "Ramble On, "Communication Breakdown." And it's a safe bet that Greta Van Fleet took that hint and ran with it.

There is no denying that Greta Van Fleet sound very much like Led Zeppelin: That Robert Plant bluesy wail/scream as reproduced to the octave by Josh Kiszka. Jimmy Page's apocalyptic, thundering guitar riffs paid proper homage by guitarist Jake Kiszka. If Greta Van Fleet fell on you, they would break every bone in your body. Just like Led Zeppelin did. Get the picture?

Greta Van Fleet, whether they want to admit it or not, drank heavily of the Led Zeppelin musical Kool-Aid, especially their legendary first album with the burning Hindenburg on the cover, which will heretofore referred to as *Led Zeppelin 1*. Zeppelin singer Robert Plant has said as much in several interviews, acknowledging that the Josh Kiszka sounds very much like him and that Greta Van Fleet's sound is very much *Led Zeppelin 1*.

Greta Van Fleet has heard it to the point of dreading it and, on occasion, getting downright pissed off about it, doing their best in countless interviews to downplay or dance around the obvious influence. But let's not be too quick to condemn, for the reality is that Greta Van Fleet is quite simply the latest of a long line of musicians who have taken their influences to creative heart and run with them.

There are the obvious sources in the blues. The Willie Dixons, the B.B. Kings, the Robert Johnsons and a whole lot of legendary blues and soul brothers. Toss a dart in any direction, let's say, generously, from Elvis forward, and it's easy to confirm that from The Beatles, The Rolling Stones, The Animals, Them, most recently The Black Crowes, ad infinitum, have added to the cause. The blues have been the father and mother to us all. So that the genre gave birth to Greta Van Fleet should come as no surprise. It's simply the natural order of things.

Yes, Greta Van Fleet has taken cues, especially the lyrical, vocal and instrumental bombast, from Led Zeppelin and, in particular, *Led Zeppelin 1*, which easily puts them in B.B.'s and Blind Willie's creative back pocket. But a case could just as easily be made that Led Zeppelin became the natural extension of that '60s British powerhouse The Yardbirds, who would regularly turn three-minute singles into commercial works of rocking art on the strength of such songs as "For Your Love," "Heart Full Of Soul, "Evil Hearted You" and "I'm A Man." But dig deeper, into such ambitious heavy blues outings as "Shapes Of Things," "Happenings Ten Years Time Ago" and a monster of a live workout on "Smokestack Lighting," and it is easy to see that a new, heavier model of The Yardbirds would be in the offing at some point in the future.

Could the highly underappreciated American band Montrose, which according to music lore, was created as an American counter to the impending invasion of Led Zeppelin (and who were responsible for such heavy FM rock staples as "Rock The Nation," "Rock Candy" and "Bad Motor Scooter") be a link in Greta Van Fleet's lineage? Check out the sonics and guitar dynamics, especially on their deeper cuts, and it's safe to say that this group of youngsters, most likely thanks to their cool musical parents, may have had Montrose on the brain as an early musical touchstone as well.

And while we're name dropping, one can toss in Captain Beyond, Cream, Black Sabbath, The Who and just about any band worthy of hard and heavy blues, and it's more than likely than not that Greta Van Fleet heard a lot that inspired them in their journey to the hottest thing currently on the heavy rock scene.

Legendary Led Zeppelin guitarist Jimmy Page hasn't out and said he had a particular bone to pick with Greta Van Fleet. The main reason is that, some years earlier, he had even bigger fish to fry when he attacked what he considered an even more blatant Led Zeppelin rip off band, Germany's Kingdom Come, who would literally steal Led Zeppelin's music, riff by riff and note by note, and pass it off as their own. "Obviously it can get to a point where it gets past being a compliment and it can be rather annoying," Page said in a *Rock Band of Los Angeles.com* piece.

Long story short, don't give all the credit and/or blame to Led Zeppelin for the burden Greta Van Fleet will most likely never shake. But there's a lot to the story behind the rise of Greta Van Fleet, the Michigan-born and bred youngsters, beyond the fact of who they sound like. There are the time-honored elements: hard work, drive and determination, the blood, sweat and tears that goes into the making of... well a Greta Van Fleet, and such immediately enticing and inspiring heavy with a capital H music as

iii

"Highway Tune," "Safari Song," "When The Curtain Falls," "You're The One" and "Black Smoke Rising."

In considering Greta Van Fleet, there is also a sense of mortality in the timeline. We're all going to die, and that includes rock icons. Most of the identifiable hard rock and heavy metal legends are well into their '70s as this book goes to press. If you've arrived at a certain age, the chances are you've seen quite a few of them pass. But there is something in the metal psyche that hopes that a new generation will rise up and take their place in a genre that, while not dead, has certainly been dangling on the precipice.

Hence the pressure already being visited on Greta Van Fleet to lead the charge into the next millennium. In interviews, the band has addressed the possibility of bringing heavy rock into the future. Their responses often rang with pretentiousness, but, and perhaps more telling, of the hopes and dreams of youth. How it will all play out will ultimately be best left to future historians and the ages.

For this author, Greta Van Fleet's hard work is most certainly at the core of this book. The band's efforts, plus a dash of determination and a dollop of passion, has resulted in a rapid rise into the public consciousness. Greta Van Fleet has only been on the radar for three years, far too early, say many purists, to justify a biography. Purists may have a point. The band members are babes in the woods, barely out of their diapers and more than a little naïve when it comes to experiencing the world. But what justifies a book on Greta Van Fleet? Try tenacity, persistence and the will to get it done and get it right. In its own way, *Hard Work: The Greta Van Fleet Story* is a hard-bitten, realistic coming-of-age story in which youth ventures out into the great unknown and is ultimately served. This is not *Hammer of the Gods*, that legendary tome that reeks of Led Zeppelin's depravity and excess. In that sense, Greta Van Fleet are Led Zeppelin of a new age, a bit more refined and glossy, yet rough and ready where it counts.

When I agreed to tackle *Hard Work: The Greta Van Fleet Story*, my journalism background was paramount. I was a hard rock and heavy metal journalist for years, when the likes of *Hit Parader, The L.A. Weekly, Zoo World, Rock Around The World, Phonograph Record Magazine, The Los Angeles Herald Examiner* and *The Orange County Register* were paying my rent and putting food on the table. I saw some of the biggest bands in the genre start their careers playing hole-in-the-wall's like The Starwood and The Whisky A-Go-Go, much like the early days of Greta Van Fleet, when biker parties and dives were the order of the day. I've seen good bands with a mountain of potential die a sad death, and I've witnessed bands make it to the top whose combined talent could fit on the head of a thimble. And I learned a few things along the way.

The high points in the history of hard rock and heavy metal have typically risen up from the depths at a time when the genre was barely a blip on the scene. Disco was reigning supreme when Led Zeppelin and Grand Funk Railroad were slugging it out in the trenches. The same is true with Greta Van Fleet. When this band came into being, rap and hip-hop was at its apex of commercial appeal, dominating the radio waves, the charts and awards season. Record labels were not falling all over themselves to sign a band they felt had limited commercial appeal.

Growing up, the members of what would become Greta Van Fleet would often be shunned as uncool and unhip by friends and classmates because all they listened to was old blues guys, while the rest of the world was blissing out to Kanye West, Ludacris and the prefabricated white pop of Maroon 5. But they stood tall in the face of the putdowns and stuck to their guns.

And so Greta Van Fleet set out to prove the naysayers wrong.

They played anywhere and everywhere that had a stage and a sound system. House parties, small clubs. Even bars when the proprietors were not checking ID's. Sometimes the audience could be counted in single digits. But there has been no compromise in this band. Like their predecessors, Greta Van Fleet forced people and record conglomerates alike to sit up and take notice.

And they kicked in the door to acceptance on a worldwide level.

This book entailed research; a whole lot of it. Some people were willing to talk. Some were reluctant to go public and on the record. Some never responded to interview queries. In the biography writing business, it was all pretty much par for the course.

As always, there were countless hours spent sifting through news articles, interviews, reviews and all manner of information. As was befitting a young and enthusiastic band, the members of Greta Van Fleet have been very press friendly. They talked to the expected big-time press, but gave equal time to the 'zines, the metal mags and even a school paper or two. Regardless of the source, information gleaned was never less than enlightening or informative, be it *Psychology Today* or *Metal Sucks.com*. There was a lot to digest and make sense of. And in the end, it did.

Greta Van Fleet are not another *American Idol*

creation. Their music is too radical, rebellious and not safe enough for that pre-fab world. They are everything that has not made their travels easy. But ultimately their journey has been rewarded.

Hard Work: The Greta Van Fleet Story is just that.

Marc Shapiro, 2019

Introduction

Tour Buses, Hotels, Shows, Repeat

It's 2019. But for Greta Van Fleet, it may as well have been 2017 or 2018. Because in the best possible way, the recent history of the brothers Kiszka (Josh, Jake and Sam) and long-time friend Danny Wagner has been nothing if not predictable. And in the best possible way.

Endless touring. Seemingly never-ending bus rides. Hotels conspicuous by their sameness. Recording. Repeat.

Like just about every aspect of their life and career, Greta Van Fleet's response to these brand-new rock 'n' roll experiences and their rapid rise to the top has been tinged with irony, humor and an exuberance that reflects on youth in transition to something much bigger than themselves. "I think we're built for this job," Josh told *Local Spins.com*. "We're not picky about where we sleep and we love the traveling. It's the best job in the world but it can be very taxing."

But however they try to explain or justify it, the watch word for Greta Van Fleet taking one giant step for hard rock kind is that every waking moment is now so damned new.

"There are times you literally wake up and have no idea where you are," reflected Josh in a 2019 interview with *Forbes.com* "It's exhausting and non- stop." Jake saw things pretty much the same way in the same interview when he offered that the last few years had been "long and difficult." But it remained for Dan to sum up Greta Van Fleet's current state of agony and ecstasy when he enthusiastically told the *Forbes.com* interviewer that "I'm 19 and I'm in this crazy world."

A world made all the more crazy by the fact that rock stardom has come upon this Frankenmuth, Michigan band so unbelievably fast. Overnight success for bands like Greta Van Fleet rarely comes so quickly. Literal babes in the woods, often in their own candid opinion, the members of Greta Van Fleet, whose youngest players are just barely out of high school and whose oldest players cannot legally drink in most of the places they've played, know enough to realize that hard rock and heavy metal groups rarely come out of nowhere. Because they've been raised on cool rock 'n' roll stories and have heard all the music that dots the i's in their world and they are not naïve to the nature of the rock 'n' roll beast.

There are years in the proverbial trenches of low- or no-paying gigs, long stretches of seemingly no progress and, perhaps even worse, no perceived success. The result? The vast majority of bands pack it in well shy of any recognition, let alone celebrity. The mortality rate for loud rock bands has been high over the years and, with rap and hip-hop the music of the moment in radio and internet outlets, the whiplash-rapid rise of Greta Van Fleet has been all the more amazing, with the band members alternately questioning and expressing sheer wonder at their impact.

"It was only a couple of days ago that I had the realization that what we are doing here is significant,"

Josh offered in a *Classic Rock* interview. "It's the idea that maybe we're introducing a new generation to rock and roll." In the same interview, Sam remained largely flummoxed in the face of it all. "It's happened faster than anybody expected. It keeps catching me off guard."

Jason Flom, who signed the band to his Lava Records label on the strength of a rough demo tape without seeing the band live, seemed to have a more practiced response to why Greta Van Fleet has struck a chord in the *Classic Rock* piece. "There hasn't been a real breakout rock band with a Capital R in a long time. With Greta Van Fleet, it's just a bunch of guys with guitars, bass and drums. It's pure."

And as their all-too-brief resume indicates, with two EP's and one album, Greta Van Fleet has struck a nerve with fans starved for the hard and heavy sounds of classic rock 'n' roll, and is being built on the time-honored precepts of lots of touring and taking their live sound to the streets and to the people. To be certain, there's a lot that rings slightly gimmicky and a bit hokey about the band. Young kids born eons after the fact paying homage to a band and a sound long considered legendary. But for those willing to dig deep beneath the hype and hoopla, there is nothing gimmicky about it.

There are just as many adults who remember The Who, Hendrix and Led Zeppelin as there are youngsters and Gen X'ers who were not born in the '60s, who are instinctively drawn to music that is hard, heavy and passionate who are flocking to Greta Van Fleet. Some consider them saviors, others throwbacks to a harder and heavier age. The bottom line is that Greta Van Fleet are not only viable at this time and place, but legitimate practitioners as well.

Jake touched on that notion in a conversation with *AntiHero Magazine*. He was in lockstep with the consensus of dealing with sudden success when he acknowledged, "I think we've taken all this quite well. A lot has happened to us in such a short span of time." And he quickly stated the reason for the success: "We've put our heart and soul into our music and people have reacted to it."

Greta Van Fleet had been kicking around since 2012, evolving from a hobby to a hometown favorite to a regional attraction and beyond. Chances are if you were a regular in the likes of Jan's Bar and Grill, Cork Pine Eatery or White's Bar, you caught their act, teens belting out Bad Company, Cream and Ozzy Osbourne covers with the occasional original like "Highway Tune" thrown in for good measure, and thought they were entertaining bordering on cool. But at that point nobody had clue as to what five years on would bring.

Long story short, Greta Van Fleet gets noticed, gets signed and records an EP entitled *Black Smoke Rising*, which spawned the single "Highway Tune," which ended up topping the *Billboard* Mainstream Rock Charts for four weeks.

Along the way, the tune, which encapsulated the heavy stomp and majesty of 1968 as filtered through Hendrix, The Who and, lest we forget, Zeppelin, had an immediate impact on the internet, with 2.6 million streams on Spotify and 1.6 million views of the accompanying video on YouTube. All of which primed the pump for a string of sell-out headlining shows. The sudden eruption of interest continued to leave the members of Greta Van Fleet somewhat in the dark.

"It ("Highway Tune") garnered attention faster

than any of us thought it would," Josh reflected in a *Billboard* conversation. "I don't know why people are connecting to it. The resounding appreciation is surreal and humbling."

Greta Van Fleet had its first taste of stardom. By the end of 2017, a second EP entitled *From the Fires* proved that this group of very young musicians had some very old and very traditional hard rock sensibilities. The result was that *From the Fires* sold more than 104,000 copies in a matter of months. If you blinked you missed what happened next.

The band made live performing bones by opening for Bob Seger and The Foo Fighters, the latter show seeing the band bring a rain-soaked crowd to its feet with a thundering performance that ended with a great Keith Moon moment when drummer Dan kicked over his drum kit. Good word of mouth made its way to no less a rock god than Elton John, who invited the band to perform at his A-list post Academy Awards party, and to jam with the superstar on the songs "Saturday Night's Alright for Fighting" and "You're The One." The group's legitimacy in the music industry was solidified when the EPs *Black Smoke Rising* and *From the Fires* were nominated for a total of four Grammys in various rock music categories.

"We didn't expect that we'd get any nominations at all," Josh chuckled in a *KROQ* radio interview. "I woke up at two in the afternoon and I had like a thousand texts. I thought the Pope had died."

Going into 2019, Greta Van Fleet, in the best possible way, have not had a chance to take a breath. In October 2018, the band released their first full-length album, *Anthem of the Peaceful Army* and, in January

2019, cemented their growing reputation as a worldwide attraction by appearing as the musical guest on *Saturday Night Live*. Needless to say, their accomplishments had, by this time, pulled way ahead of the Led Zeppelin knocks and the band members were going numb at the constant questions about how fast things had come their way. But always cordial when it came to the media, Sam gave it another shot in a conversation with *The 405*.

"We've packed so much into the past year that it's felt like three years. But everything that has happened to us has gone by so quickly that it feels more like three months."

Shortly after the band's *Saturday Night Live* appearance, it was announced that Greta Van Fleet would embark on a truly monster international six-month concert tour that would include major appearances in Europe as well as North America. Barely over the legal limit in so many aspects of their personal lives, Greta Van Fleet were now taking a mighty step in the direction of professional adulthood. And they continue to be in awe of their accomplishments.

"It's an amazing excuse for a career," Sam told *Glide Magazine* during an interview in which he seemed hard pressed to hide a smirk of satisfaction. "We get to see all these beautiful places and amazing faces. It's an amazing thing."

Chapter One

My Kind of Frankenmuth Is

Frankenmuth is not a myth. There actually is such a place. But chances are if you're not familiar with the ins and outs of Michigan and the subtle and unexpected twists of the state's superhighway system, you might have driven right past the town and not even noticed.

And that would be too bad.

Because Frankenmuth, located in a hub of a detour between the more well-known cites of Flint, where the likes of Grand Funk Railroad reigned supreme, and Saginaw north of Detroit where Motown became legend and the MC5 and Mitch Ryder and The Detroit Wheels left their mark, is a city out of time. Frankenmuth is a kitschy, Andy of Mayberry sitcom fairyland of all things German. Founded in 1845 by a group of German Lutheran missionaries and known to this day as 'Michigan's Little Bavaria,' Frankenmuth, despite claiming farming at its primary economic core, is for all intents a tourist destination, playing up German food, history and festivals.

Frankenmuth is Middle America to the max, a place where old fashioned is emblazoned on the resident's psyches. Values tend to run to traditional and conservative with a rarely seen underpinning of liberal. It's a place where everybody knows everybody, relationships are lasting and attitudes are defended to the death. In other words, Frankenmuth is a place that people never leave and if they do, they usually come back.

If you dial the telephone number 1-800-Funtown, you will have discovered the real reason Frankenmuth has been a must-see for decades. Sam recalled the town in a conversation with *The Spectrum*. "Yeah it's a pretty fun place. There's always a festival going on. It's a beautiful little town based on Bavarian architecture."

Frankenmuth, whose population hovers right around 5,200, is quite successful at marketing their German heritage and has always been, in the best possible way, a one-trick pony called Tourist.

By regional standards, their annual Oktoberfest Celebration is considered one of the best and musical and theatrical productions at Fischer Hall and the town's annual Auto Fest are must-sees. Annually, more than three million tourists manage to find Frankenmuth and revel in the Disneyland-meets-small-town-America quaintness of its streets, town and shops. Bronner's Christmas Wonderland is a monster of a superstore, their eateries, such as Zehnder's, are notorious for tasty chicken, and many of the businesses and attractions around town proudly boast the word "Bavarian" in their name.

Dan was enthusiastic as he played public relations man for Frankenmuth in conversation with *The Spectrum*. "There's a river running through the center of town. There's boat rides, a wooden bridge, horse carriage rides and fudge. Frankenmuth has the best fudge in the world."

But in all candor, Frankenmuth has never been what one would call the ground zero of rock 'n' roll.

Occasionally cover bands would play the hits at house parties and school dances, and there was a smattering of local musicians who would moonlight from their day jobs by entertaining the locals at nearby parks or get-togethers. But the closest thing to a discernible rock scene was what the town elders proudly christened Family Fun Night, where the occasional non-threatening combo would play the hits for dining and dancing pleasure.

Frankenmuth is also the place that helped mold the soul and spirit of the members of Greta Van Fleet. No town is totally crime-free, but Frankenmuth has always been pretty damned close. There were the usual juvenile high jinks, but it was rarely serious enough to get the law out in a lights and sirens way. The closest thing to any law enforcement presence was the occasional police and fire department vehicles leading an annual parade down Main Street.

Sam reflected on the town in a conversation with *Bangs.com* when he offered, "Frankenmuth was a great place to grow up in, in just about every way. The town is rich in history. There is so much untouched forests and land around there. Our souls have always run wild in Frankenmuth."

Likewise, Josh maintains a love affair with the town, as he explained in a *Huffington Post* interview. "I think it [the town] is kind of romantic in a traditional sense. It's a tight community and a wonderful community, filled with genuine, loving people, real supportive people. The town is like all good things. It's like a picture perfect, Americana sort of thing."

In a *Bullet Music.com* interview, Danny was philosophical, and at times, poetic in discussing the place he called home, explaining how the vibe of the town stood

3

out from the preconceived notion of a wild and wooly Michigan. "We come from an area that doesn't really fit in with a lot of the rest of the cities in Michigan. We grew up in a very rural countryside. A lot of woods, a lot of grains, a lot of farm fields and a lot of rivers and streams." Sam in *Bullet* put the love affair between the band and their roots in perspective when he simply said, "It was a great place to grow up."

But the image of days gone by has undergone a metamorphosis of sorts with the advent of Greta Van Fleet. All the old fashioned, time-honored niceties are still in place. But with the success of Greta Van Fleet, the local kids who are making good as rock stars around the world, the landscape of the simple times has changed and brought a measure of notoriety to the formerly sleepy town of Frankenmuth.

Along the streets and storefronts, the mood is now one of quiet excitement and a sense of pride in a town where everybody knows everybody. As word has spread of the band and their hometown, Frankenmuth has suddenly become front-page news. There's a new kind of tourist in town; younger, hipper, with longer hair and musically inclined, descending on the hamlet to seek out the local rock 'n' roll stars. And if the band was not around to do an interview, just about everybody else in town was.

Brittany Dukarski, a long-time Frankenmuth resident, explained the change in an interview with *The Advertiser*. "The mood in town is very hyped up. A lot of people come to see them (the band) or to be in the town that they came from. They want to see where the members of Greta Van Fleet have hung out, where they grew up and to learn about their origin story."

The Greta Van Fleet story began at birth.

Jake and Josh Kiszka were born five minutes apart on April 23, 1996. Sam Kiszka was born on April 3, 1999. Danny Wagner was born on December 29, 1998. But even before they arrived, their parents were already laying the musical groundwork.

"When we were not even born yet, our father was playing stuff," Sam told *Sing Me A Song.com*. "The blues, rhythm and blues, soul music. We came into the world having already heard all the good stuff."

Chapter Two

Smart House

Kelly and Karen Kiszka are well-read, educated and intellectually inclined. Outgoing and salt of the earth, they were easy to get to know and comfortable in any social setting. They have never been a couple to flaunt those qualities. To the people in and around Frankenmuth, they have always been just laid-back folks.

People know Kelly as a chemist and Karen as a science teacher. But beyond that, one would have to dig fairly deep, for the parents of Jake, Josh and Sam Kiszka tend to keep much to themselves—and to select family and friends. Anyone looking for a hint of attitude, philosophy or a clue as to just what makes them tick might do well to start with their bookshelves.

Scan a shelf and you're liable to find Frederick Nietzsche, Jean Paul Sartre, John Steinbeck, Thoreau and Ralph Waldo Emerson. There are also titles by Allen Ginsberg, Aldous Huxley and Ernest Hemingway to consider. If that were not enough, there are also books by Hunter S. Thompson and *National Lampoon Magazine*, indicating that the elder Kiszka's were way left of center when it came to attitudes and philosophies.

And when they were old enough to contemplate books, Josh, Jake and Sam instantly got it.

"My father has a bachelor's degree in philosophy and so we always had these books around," Josh recounted during an interview with *Prohbtd.com*. "So naturally we were drawn to what was inside them. We were always surrounded by challenging thoughts and ideas."

Josh would recall in *Loudersound.com* that their book learning, as well as the family's progressive bent, was geared toward the concept of individuality, and that even the hint of something that went against the parent's notion of what true freedom was became a no-no for the Kiszka boys. "There were things our father warned us to be careful with. Nietzsche was somebody he warned us about. He wouldn't let us read certain texts at all."

It was an aesthetic of free expression that was passed down to the Kiszka sons. Conversations over the dinner table often evolved into spirited and freewheeling give-and-take in which both sides of any given topic were enthusiastically debated. But the anti- establishment—often bordering on Beat and hippie—aesthetics often resulted in the laying down of certain unorthodox laws. By all accounts, the children were not allowed to watch television. And while music was definitely at the forefront, what with Kelly a noted local musician who played guitar, bass and what has been described in many quarters as a "dirty" harmonica (and a family musical tree that includes the talents of an older daughter, an uncle and grandparents), there were some restrictions. And the biggest no-no was pop music.

"We have always been into the blues, classic rock and all those kinds of sounds," Karen related to *The Advertiser*. "That's what we always listened to when the kids were growing up. They weren't allowed to listen to pop music because we didn't like most of it."

But the trade-off for the Kiszka boys was unlimited access to a cellar full of vinyl, a literal wonderland of sounds. Much has been made of the wide variety of music the boys were exposed to, and to chronicle the entire family collection would be exhausting. Some examples suffice in terms of the diversity of music they were exposed to at an early age: Robert Johnson, Son House, Muddy Waters, Lightnin' Hopkins, Albert King, BB King, John Lee Hooker, The Beatles, Bob Dylan, The Who and John Denver. To this day, the members of Greta Van Fleet remain in awe of those records and, by turns, are often at a loss to name specific influences but rather marvel at the influences of the whole collection.

"There are so many things that were introduced to us growing up," reflected Jake in a *Premier Guitar.com* conversation. "Despite what people might think, it wasn't just Led Zeppelin. It's The Beatles, the whole British Invasion, American blues, soul and roots music. There was a pretty broad range of influences that we grew up with."

Given Greta Van Fleet's guitar heavy approach, it will come as a surprise to many rock and metal musicologists that a major influence on the band has been John Denver, as explained by Sam in *Premier Guitar.com*. "John Denver was a huge factor for us growing up. Our dad and uncle and everybody around us would play John Denver all the time. For us, it was kind of freedom music."

Josh and Jake tended to work out their musical priorities as only young children can. When driving in the family car, it was not uncommon for the boys to break into song. From the outset, Josh had the more commanding vocals and Jake had, for all intents and purposes, latched onto the guitar as his childhood choice.

Being essentially toddlers, there was no pressure

about cultivating serious musical interests, and it is to Kelly and Karen's credit that nothing was ever forced upon their children. Yes, music was a big part of their life experience, but the sheer normalcy of their life lifestyle—hanging out with friends, exploring the nearby woods and nature and, well, just being children—took precedence. But it was soon evident that Jake had taken to the guitar and that his father was a constant influence on his choices. Jake who painted a picture of his father as a saint in conversation with *Zebra Magazine*.

"Our dad's in two bands and he's a blues harmonica player. And so all of us pay respect to growing up in a creatively nurturing environment where we just sort of grew up playing music. My dad would show us musical things, blues records when we were really young, too young to even get the blues. But there's a special element to being that young and listening to that music. It can touch your soul."

Not only was their introduction to timeless music a natural indoctrination but it was a no- pressure situation. Music, through the gentle hands of Kelly and Karen, was an easy state of affairs, designed to listen, enjoy and, yes, to maybe learn. Sam recalled that fact when exploring his early experiences in conversation with *Columbus Calling*.

"Our parents never pushed music on us. It was never like 'Here! You're going to like this.' But when were in the car or just around the house, there was always music playing. It would be Sam and Dave, or Joe Cocker, the old blues guys like Elmore James and Howling Wolf, the classic stuff like The Beatles and The Allman Brothers. The music was always there. We'd put all those songs on a disc and play it out in the yard when we were playing. Sometimes we'd go into the garage and go through our dad's vinyl collection. I'm sure we scratched up a few of his albums but it was fun times."

And at a very early age, the Kiszka boys became particular. With pop music radio stations forbidden in the Kiszka household, it remained for the kids to learn about the genre from the outside world. Sam recalled his first experience with that alien music form.

"When we were in the first grade and riding the school bus, the local pop music radio station was always on. We'd be listening to that stuff and we were like 'What is this? Who would want to listen to this?'"

Jake would echo Sam's sentiments, conceding that the music they were introduced to was more the luck of the draw than anything else. "It all boiled down to just what we were listening to when we were younger," he told *Pop Matters.com*. "It didn't seem to us that it was a particular kind of music. It was just what we had."

Once Jake stopped crawling all over his dad's instruments that were scattered around the house and actually picked one up and attempted to play, he was learning from square one on the guitar. His first guitar was acoustic, your basic beginner's model. Jake would be diligent in mastering basic chords and was soon attempting to pick out songs by the likes of Bob Dylan and Jimi Hendrix. The rule of the house was simple. As Jake would reach a level of proficiency, his father would reward him with an update to a slightly better guitar. Barely into elementary school and, with a steadily increasing number of hard work influences in his head, Jake began fantasizing about his first electric guitar. But the final decision would, as always, remain with his father.

But that did not mean that Kelly would not begin to steer him in that direction. Shortly after Jake turned eight, father and son had a moment, sitting down in the living room to watch an old VHS copy of a documentary on the rock power trio Cream. Jake sat transfixed as he watched the group, and especially guitarist Eric Clapton, run through explosive blues hits and standards. And as he would recall in a *Music Radar.com* interview, that was when he had an emotional breakthrough.

"I saw Eric Clapton and I was blown away by his presence. Looking at him and seeing this sense of purpose, I turned to my dad right then and there and said, 'That's who I want to be!'"

Chapter Three

Getting Real

By the time Jake and Josh Kiszka turned 8, their musical attitudes were in transition. Kelly and Karen continued to offer up music as an option, still hanging onto the last fragments of 'it's a phase and they'll grow out of it,' yet sensing it was becoming a bit more. And if the Kiszka brothers were being honest, their musical education at that point was nothing more than a hoot or a hobby.

But there was a new attitude on the horizon; the boys were not growing out of it. If anything, they were becoming more dedicated, eager and anxious. Music at age 8 was morphing into the possibilities of a career. Or what passed for one in the mind of a child.

The band members would readily acknowledge in later years that Bob Dylan's *Blood on the Tracks* album was a turning point as Sam related in a conversation with *Newsday*. "I found Dylan's *Blood on the Tracks* album in the basement and the song "Tangled Up In Blue" blew my mind. The lyricism of that song was incredible. I really wanted to understand that song. From then on, I was always in the basement, usually with Jake, and we would sit and listen to Bob Dylan while we would paint or draw. There is just something about Bob Dylan. Dylan really inspired us to think about music."

And then there would be those annual winter vacations the family took to a camp called Yankee Springs, where true music magic occurred. Yankee Springs is an out-of-the-way campground that long ago had become a very hippie-like gathering of the musical tribes in which the Kiszka's would meet up with like-minded family and friends for a days-long musical experience. People would bring all manner of instruments and spontaneous musical jams would break out at all hours of the day and night. It was all very tribal, a communion of nature and creativity in its most simplistic form. If this were the '60 s it might well be considered a hippie gathering. The reality was that it was a group of musicians bent on exploring music in all possible ways. And for the Kiszka children, it was eye-opening nirvana.

Josh was brimming over with enthusiasm when he spoke of the Yankee Springs experience with *Sing Me A Song.com*. "Every year was better than Christmas. In the evenings or during the day there was always somebody making music. Everybody was getting together, experimenting with sounds and having fun making music." Likewise, Jake would have his eyes opened wide by the experience. "It's really awe inspiring when you see this completely surrealistic environment, to see all these people from all over the place come together and realize that what brought them together was music."

But while notions of what music could be were always in their young children's world, the Kiszka parents, despite sensing real possibilities in their children's evolving talents, continued to be matter of fact when it came to their boys' musical education." Our family was always very casual about music," Sam told *Bangs.com*. "They just liked it and the music they played.

Our parents were not stern. They were just very encouraging about everything."

Jake echoed Sam's attitude, pointing out that their earliest inclination to play music rested very much in their upbringing, telling *Listen Iowa.com*, "Growing up in an artistic environment gave us a unique perspective. Growing up in a family that was musically inclined and with their friends being so artistically and musically inclined, being surrounded by all that, was certainly influential."

However, in their own way, the Kiszka brothers were being gently guided down a progressive path, heavy on the subtlety as exemplified by the learning curve proffered by Jake's father. "I played this little acoustic guitar seemingly forever but when I started wanting to play electric guitar, my dad laid down some rules. When I learned certain songs on an acoustic, songs by Hendrix, Bob Seger, Gordon Lightfoot and Bob Dylan, then I could upgrade to an electric. Looking back on that, it was a process of not only learning how to play but to learn how to play with subtlety."

The Frankenmuth School District had always been a model in progressive education. Students were taught the three R's, but the curriculum was rife with creative encouragement and outside the box thinking. Consequently, it would be shortly after turning 8 and finding his muse in Eric Clapton, that Jake had a true "come to Jesus'" moment courtesy of his fourth grade teacher who, one day, decided to shake things up a little bit by enlightening her class to a bit of music from her generation.

"I was in the fourth grade and our teacher decided to play us Jimi Hendrix's version of the "Star Spangled Banner," Jake told *Music Radar.com*. "I remember that most of the kids in the classroom didn't get it but, for me, something really clicked. I get goosebumps now just thinking about it. I remember tearing up because the music was just so emotional. For the next three years, I became obsessed with Hendrix."

Word travelled fast in a town like Frankenmuth. And word of the Kiszka brothers and their obsession with rock and blues was making the rounds.

Consequently, it was not long before everybody within Frankenmuth were familiar with the Kiszka kids musical skills. Some in the neighborhood were so bold as to come by the Kiszka home to observe the kids at play. One of those with a front row seat was Eric Clauder, band director of the Frankenmuth School District, who related to *ABC 12* that, "All of those four gentlemen had immense talent as they came through our schools. It was really noticeable, a lot of improvisational skills, just natural talent. You could hand any of those guys an instrument and they would be able to pick it up really quick."

Jake was not the only one obsessed. While the entire Kiszka clan seemed to be deeply intellectually inclined and well-spoken when it came to music, by the time the twin Kiska brothers entered high school, a strong case could be made that Josh might, creatively, have Jake by a nose.

To wit: Josh has always been acknowledged as a voracious reader, especially when it came to Beats and more progressive older poets and writers. If a question regarding Proust or Hemingway came up as a *Jeopardy* question, Josh would most likely ring in first. While he definitely knows his music and was often inspired by its possibilities, he was not all-in by the time he reached his teens.

"I never really saw music on the horizon in terms of a career," he remarked to *The Huffington Post.* "I had a lot of other interests prior to considering a singing career. I liked the idea of acting. I did all kinds of acting in local community theater. I wanted to be a writer of books and film. I even considered being a comedian for a while. But most of all, I wanted to be a filmmaker. As soon as I discovered film at a young age, it transformed my perspective on most things because, with film, you could tell a story."

Consequently, during his teen years, it was Josh who became a minor celebrity on the Frankenmuth creative scene. He was a literal filmmaking dynamo, always writing, always casting, always filming on a reported 30 films, ranging in budgets from zero to a reported $8,000. Josh's big hit came at age 15 when he entered the Riverside Saginaw Film Festival challenge to write, cast and produce a five-minute film in 72 hours. Josh's film, entitled *Smiley Face Bomb*, a gritty exercise in which a group of waitresses takes matters into their own hands when society treats them badly, earned Josh plaudits for its intensity and professional quality work.

Josh would relive the joys of filmmaking in a *Mlive.com* interview. "It was pretty intense. The crazy part was getting by on seven or eight hours sleep and staying up until five in the morning to get everything done. I got 35 of my friends, including my brother Jake, to get this done. I will absolutely do it again. It was crazy, fun, truly a great experience."

As was his time as a member of the Frankenmuth Community Theater. Josh had a knack for the dramatic and, at a very young age, appeared to be a natural actor, a talent he most certainly learned as a budding rock 'n' roll front man. He was a regular in all the Community Theater productions, his most triumphant moment, according to those who witnessed Josh on stage, was the lead in the production of *Willy Wonka And The Chocolate Factory*. Josh remembered that play in conversation with *MLive.com*. "There was a psychedelic rock vibe to it. We played three nights playing to packed houses. For me, that was dead on. It was a blast."

Around the time Josh was having his "great experience," Jake was experiencing his own life-changing moment, and it was anything but good.

"I was in the eighth grade and just being a kid. I was rough housing with a friend, wrestling, when I broke my arm," he painfully recalled to *Fender.com*. "I freaked out. I was scared that I would never play guitar again. Three days after I broke it, I had surgery and ended up having to wear a cast for about six months. I would go down in the basement and try to play but, with the cast on, it was tough. At the advice of my doctor, in an attempt to strengthen the muscles in my hand, I went into our shed and sanded off the underside of the cast near my hand while keeping the back of the cast on."

Jake's arm healed and it was with a sigh of relief that he found he could once again play and, owing to a plate that was put in his arm, was able to add an additional fret to his playing style. It must have seemed like a favor from God, and the youngster used this brush-with- fate moment to start taking his musical skills in a more serious direction.

By the time he turned 16, Jake seemed totally immersed in the idea of music as an avocation and set about laying down roots for his future. This led to the Kiszka family garage. Until that point, Jake's formal introduction to a band concept had been as guitarist for the Frankenmuth High School Jazz Band, which may or may not have whet his appetite with musicians and music other than his brothers or, perhaps, was his attempt to recreate the Yankee Springs experience in his own yard. Jake was looking for something spontaneous. And that's when the Kiszka jams began.

"That's kind of when we started going out to the garage," Jake told *The Illinois Entertainer*. "To that point I had been in jazz band, playing guitar, and another friend who had just transferred into the school district, Kyle Hauck, was into music as well. I brought him back to our house and we started playing after school."

The garage get-together started out as a loosely constructed jam session. But as news spread along the Frankenmuth word-of-mouth hotline, the jams became the hot place for people to be. Josh popped in and out, and would add what would be very Zeppelin-like vocals. Kyle was a regular on drums, as Sam would recall, years later in an interview with *The Sydney Morning Herald*. "People would start coming over to hang out and listen to us screw around in the garage. It was just a second nature kind of thing. Everybody was just playing guitar, and eventually, that's what started us out wanting to be musicians."

For most, it was just a kick, a chance to hang out and hear their friends play. But it soon became evident that a core group of musicians; Jake, Josh and, to a lesser degree, Kyle, were beginning to take things seriously. This brought about the first bouts of disagreement, compromise and raised the issue of getting along with others. These informal garage jams also saw the first flowering of creative talent from Josh and Jake.

Josh had been a slow but steady convert to the British

Invasion style of heavy blues rock and, by high school, was only beginning to come in contact with Led Zeppelin and lead singer Robert Plant's screaming vocal style. It was a style that would make its appearance during a moment of frustration during those early jam sessions. "Josh was singing but was struggling to be heard over the musicians," Jake recalled in *Rolling Stone*. "At one point, he let out these very Led Zeppelin style shrieks. We all just stopped playing and were like 'Whatever you just did, keep doing it because it sounds badass.'"

For his part, Jake was slowly evolving into a serious songwriter, crafting lyrics and sonic instrumental structures into promising musical elements. It was during those early jams, around 2010, that he stumbled upon a lick that would ultimately turn into the band's first truly original song, "Highway Tune."

"I had just started writing songs and music and was starting to build on structuring songs," Jake disclosed to *Livewire.com*. "Highway Tune" was one of the first songs I had ever written, and in those days, I was looking for a perfect riff for that song. So one day, I plugged my guitar into one of my dad's harmonica amps and sat down and worked that out. After five minutes I worked that out and I was like 'Okay. That's a riff then.'"

Those early jam sessions, grew in intensity as the core group of musicians continued to search for musical perfection. In the strictest sense of the word, this was a family and, as everybody knows, families fight. And there were those occasions when one or both of the Kiszka parents would rush to the garage at the sound of an non-musical crash or bang to find out what was going on.

Jake matter-of-factly recalled in *Alternative Nation.com* that, "Early on, there were broken doors, projectile instruments and the throwing of fists." Sam would tell *Music Connection* pretty much the same story. "In the beginning, we had lots of disagreements when we were practicing in the garage and we'd get pretty violent with each other. But that was because we were taking the music very seriously and we wanted everything to be perfect."

In time, the jam sessions evolved into a shakedown cruise in which some musicians found themselves on the same musical page, and began to click as a marginally professional unit. Josh reflected on that sudden evolution in *Listen Iowa.com* when he remembered, "Being in a band was not something I set out to particularly do. But suddenly, it all felt pretty natural."

Ever the stickler for the dramatic moment, when talking to *Billboard*, Jake played up the moment it all made sense: "Josh and I looked at each other and said, 'this is going to be something pretty substantial.'"

Chapter Four

Enter Sam Man/Enter Dan Man

Sam was leading the typical pre-teen life. Like his older siblings, he loved music and was an active participant when the Kiszka brothers tore into their dad's record collection. But while Josh and Jake were already flirting with the notion of music as an avocation, Sam was not even close to becoming serious about anything, let alone a possible life as a musician.

But, as he would explain to *Fender.com,* he was definitely aware of what was going on in his household. "There were always musicians around. My dad would always bring his musician buddies around to play. Then he and Josh and Jake would go out to the garage and jam and sing."

But while not an active participant in those early Kiszka garage sessions, Sam was around the countless volumes of vinyl that the Kiszka boys had honed their musical chops on and, like his brothers, Sam cultivated a keen interest in classic music. One of my earliest memories was discovering The Beatles and playing some of their songs on my iPod" he recalled to *Cowgirlzentertainment.com.* "After about a month of hearing those songs I was ready for something new so I found some new songs, things like "Let It Be," "Octopus Garden." "I'm Looking Through You" and so much more. It was amazing to me that all these great songs were written by The Beatles."

Musically, he was halfway there but it would remain for Sam's mother to give him a not-too-subtle push in the right direction shortly after Sam turned 12.

"My mom started telling me that I looked like a bass player," he would recall in interviews with the likes of *CBS San Francisco*, *The Cleveland Scene* and *Fender.com*. "And I was like, the reason she started saying that to me was probably because she saw the opportunity for me to do something in a band. My dad had a bass laying around and so, one day, I just started messing around with it."

With such influences as John Entwistle and Jack Bruce to guide him, Sam would spend the next year immersed in the instrument. Along the way, he discovered the joys of the bass line in "I Heard It Through The Grapevine" through endless hours listening to Motown. Not surprisingly, Sam was immediately fascinated with the idea of playing bass and was discovering his own innate abilities with the instrument along the way. But he was the first to admit that this voyage of discovery would be slow and steady. "After about a year of playing I had learned some really simple stuff."

Along the way, Sam would also get the itch to add keyboards to his repertoire. "We always had a piano around the house and I kind of got to the point where I didn't just want to be a bass player," he told *CBS San Francisco*. "But what really got me into the keyboard was The Beatles' song "She's So Heavy." That song just had this ripping organ and I thought 'Holy shit! That sounds so cool! I want to be able to do that.'"

Sam continued to practice and, according to reports, had become quite good at the bass and, to a slightly lesser degree, the keyboard. But he was still a bit leery about trying to crack the Kiszka garage jam sessions. Josh and Jake knew that Sam had been working out on the instrument and, privately, agreed that he was developing some decent chops. It would, finally, remain for his two older brothers to make the first move, as Jake recounted in *The Illinois Entertainer*. "One day Sam was on his way home from school and we stopped him and said 'Hey, you want to play bass?' So Sam came out and started playing."

Looking back on that moment, Sam told *Pollstar* that he was surprised at his brothers' inviting him into their 'club.' "Usually, for a younger brother, it's like 'Get out of here! We don't want to hang around with you!' But my brothers were so great about that. They always included me in the things that they did."

Sam fit easily into the garage/jam environment. Either directly and indirectly, he knew most of the other musicians and, with Josh and Jake seemingly ramrodding the proceedings, he did not need to catch up on the blues and heavy rock influences echoing off the walls. Among those regulars at the sessions were the occasional newcomers and semi-regulars who would pop in and out. Sam fit in easily. As did another new kid in the garage.

A childhood friend named Danny Wagner.

By small town, middle America measurements, Danny and the Kiszka brothers were literally next door neighbors. "I grew up just five miles west of them, just down the road from them," he told a *405.com* reporter. "It was like the equivalent of three country blocks. There was a creek that ran from their house to my house. If anything, we probably grew up with too much of each other."

Sam would also reference the question of distance between himself and Dan in a joke-filled conversation with *The Spectrum.com* when he offered that Daniel would have to swim up the creek from his house to get to practice. "Yeah, that creek that runs behind our house, if you go down it a few miles, you're at Daniel's."

By the time Dan entered kindergarten, he had become fast friends with the Kiszka family, often accompanying the family on various outings and camping trips. Dan and Sam became particularly tight. Being the same age gave them similar interests. And as they got older they found that much of their interests centered around music. Sam recalled in a *Grown Up Rock.com* interview that "Dan was the only guy in school I could relate to musically." Sam would elaborate on their connection in conversation with *The Spectrum.com:* "By the time we got to middle school, all the people we knew were listening to rap and hip-hop and whatever was on the local pop station. But Daniel and I were always bouncing classic rock stuff off each other."

Dan recalled that he was quite the athlete growing up, telling *Blues Rock Review*, "I grew up playing a lot of sports. I was a pretty avid golfer."

But even as a child, music was always there.

"Guitar was the first instrument I started playing when I was very young," he recalled to *Modern Drummer* and *Blues Rock Review*. "My mom kind of got me into guitar because she played when she was growing up. She was heavily into folk music and that was the stuff I grew up learning how to play. The first song I ever learned how to play was 'Puff The Magic Dragon'."

Dan was nothing if not independently minded and would chafe at the formal aspects of learning how to play an instrument. "Initially, I took lessons," he told *Modern Drummer*. "But I grew to dislike the whole idea of a schedule. So I started to play on my own and, as it turned out, drums became the first instrument I could teach myself to play."

Dan remained with the guitar but, as he entered his early teens, drums became his go-to instrument. To that point, Dan's musical education had remained a solitary pursuit. But by the time he reached middle school, there was a sudden shift in attitude. "When I was in middle school, I joined the school band. That was my first experience playing with other musicians. When you play by yourself, you set the pace," he explained to *Modern Drummer*. "All of a sudden I had to start becoming one instrument with other players."

Dan's ability to multi-task would come into play early in his high school years when he tried out for the school's jazz band. He wanted to play drums, but when he discovered the drum slot had been filled, he had no qualms about switching to guitar. By that time Dan and Sam had cemented both their friendship and their musical interests. That translated into the two friends' official musical unveiling when, with Sam on bass, Dan on guitar and friend and jam regular Kyle Hauck on drums, they played a Frankenmuth grad party as a trio going by the name of Hollywood. "It was just a one-off thing," Sam said *to Pure Grain Audio.com*. "We just basically jammed out and it was really cool."

Dan recalled how the casual lifelong relationship, most likely fueled by the chemistry in the Hollywood gig, suddenly turned into something much deeper. In a conversation with *Airplay Today.com he recalled,* "Sam and I became real good friends toward the end of middle school. We had always known each other but had never really hung out. But once we realized that we had the same taste in music, we started having this musicianship relationship. We started getting together and just playing our instruments together. One day, Sam told me how his brothers and a bunch of other people from the school would get together in his family garage and jam. He invited me over to play with everyone else. So I did and it turned out to be magical."

Chapter Five

What's in a Name?

Going into 2012, the magic emanating from the Kiszka family garage was palpable.

The jam sessions were becoming tighter and further reaching. A massive amount of original songs were being conceived, created and executed in a rapidly maturing manner. Kyle Hauck had emerged as a capable drummer, somebody who could be relied upon to produce a heavy beat. Sam had become an instant fit, moving ambitiously through the bottom sound of heavy rock. And it went without saying that Josh and Jake were pointing this group of musicians in a direction that had not been hugely favored by the public for years.

Yet for the Kiska brothers, there was nothing serious about it.

"We were just four friends who were playing around in a garage band. We just loved to get together and write songs."

Dan, continued to pop in and out of the sessions, proving his talents at both the drums and guitar while gaining points with Josh and Jake thanks to his ability to pick up on the nuances of the original songs that continued to flow at a steady pace. Dan saw that period as a hoot more than anything else, something totally laid back and not serious. "I hate using the word hobby," he told *Blues Rock Review,* "but the reality was that what we were doing was not much more than a hobby. It was barely on anybody's radar."

But word of mouth was changing all that. Musicians at the sessions and their friends soon had the Frankenmuth teenage hotline clicking in overtime. Which, in hindsight, would seem unusual because, for the longest time, the Kiska's and their, by teen standards, retro choice of music, had made the brothers odd ducks in the eyes of their pop- and rap-loving peers. But all that changed when it became known that these "musical outcasts" were getting together and playing real music. People kept wanting to know when the band was going to play and where could they see them. All of which fed into the purity and naturalness of the Kiska's and their entry into live performing.

"We loved the idea of playing in front of people and getting a reaction from them," related Jake. "And so when people started asking, we were happy to oblige. And just like that, we were a band."

Jake would be almost matter of fact that, for him, a long-time wish was about to come true. "I always wanted to put together a band but I never figured it would be a band with my brothers."

Throughout the early months of 2012, the band, so casual that they didn't even have a name, appeared at a number of house parties and school-sponsored parties and dances, playing such covers as "Crazy Train," by Ozzy Osbourne and "House Of The Rising Sun" by The Animals as well as an increasing number of original songs, including an embryonic version of "Highway Tune." In a conservative town like Frankenmuth, the band had their fingers crossed for a positive response. The kids would understand it. The parents... well, that was a different story.

"People were just freaking out," said Josh, encapsulating those early house party and grad dances in *The Detroit Metro Times*. "It was like 'Oh my God! There's so much skin and it's just too loud! It's going to blow the windows out and the whole world is going to melt!'"

Word was beginning to spread beyond the teen circle. And the town's older generation was beginning to sit up and take notice.

One adult who took a particularly keen interest in the band was Jon Webb, a family friend and the executive director of the Frankenmuth Historical Museum and an influential member of the Frankenmuth stage community. In a quote that appeared in *Alternative Nation.com*, Webb recalled observing the band in its infant stage and his reaction. "I told them they were actually pretty good but that they didn't know any songs all the way through and that Josh was making up half the words that they do sing. I told them that if they could learn ten songs all the way through with the right words, that I would see about putting them on stage."

Eventually the band fulfilled their end of the promise and cobbled together a complete set of material. Those early shows quickly turned the band into local celebrities, all the more so since three of the four band members were still in high school and readily recognizable at their lockers or wandering down the halls between classes. It would not be long before the city fathers and tastemakers got hip to what their children were talking about. That was when the band was invited to perform at the city's annual

31

outdoor car show and all-around family friendly good-time event, Auto Fest.

The band knew that Auto Fest was a big deal and that a whole lot of people would turn out. They continued to practice long and hard and were satisfied that they were ready to hit what passed for the big time in Frankenmuth. It was at that moment that they realized that they had to call themselves something. How they came up with the name Greta Van Fleet would go down in the annals of rock 'n' roll lore.

"It was a pretty big deal," Josh told *The Detroit Free Press*. "We got to thinking that we were going to need a name. Initially we came up with some crazy ideas but nothing seemed to work. We had spent all this time playing in the garage day in and day out and hadn't really thought about a name."

Josh began the story in conversation with *The Huffington Post*. "It was the day before we were set to play Auto Fest and we knew we had to come up with a name to call ourselves. Kyle had gone to lunch with his grandfather and then he was dropped off at practice."

Sam recounted the name story for *Billboard*. "Kyle came to us at practice and said that his grandpa told him that he needed to cut wood for Gretna Van Fleet (an 87-year-old great-grandmother and Frankenmuth resident who also had musical roots as a sax and piano player in a band in the '50 s). Kyle thought the name was interesting and brought it to the band at practice. We all kind of liked it and Josh suggested that we drop the 'n' out of Gretna and it would roll off the tongue better. I think it's an interesting name because it's different. You don't really know what kind of music is going to be produced by a group with that name."

As off the wall and un-rock 'n' roll sounding as Greta Van Fleet was, the origin of the name would quickly become a hook of massive proportions in telling the band's story. But not content with the conceit of "that's our story and we're sticking to it." Josh, inexplicably, would float an alternative version of the tale in an interview with *Review Magazine*. "We had been going over a lot of names and we decided to just slip open a phone book and came upon the name Gretna Ensley. We decided to take the 'n' out of Gretna and we had Greta Ensley."

Chalk the second version up to youthful exaggeration. Long story short, that version of the naming of Greta Van Fleet would never be repeated in any media outlet, and nobody in the press, to this point, has seen fit to broach the question to the band.

The decision to call the band Greta Van Fleet immediately made the rounds and the response was, to say the least, mixed. One of the most telling critiques came from band mother Karen Kiszka, who conceded to *The Advertiser* that her first reaction had not been great. "I said 'that's a lovely name but it's somebody's name and she might not appreciate that.' And it's a long name. It's not a good band name."

Word immediately got around that a heavy rock band calling themselves Greta Van Fleet would be playing Auto Fest. Fortunately, when the band's namesake grandmother found out about it, she took it well. "That won't last long," she laughed in a *Billboard* interview. "That's not a name for a band." But, as Josh remembered in *The Huffington Post*. "We did that first show as Greta Van Fleet and the name just stuck."

That first show would be a trial by jangled nerves. In

the days leading up to the appearance, the newly christened Greta Van Fleet crashed out a set of covers consisting largely of Ozzy Osbourne, Led Zeppelin and assorted big-time metal covers. "We scraped together what we'd played in the garage into what we figured would be an hour set," Jake told *The Illinois Entertainer*. "We had songs like "Smokestack Lighting," "Rolling and Tumbling," "Spoonful" and songs by Cream, Bob Dylan and Neil Young."

The band would remember sweating bullets as they loaded their equipment onto the back of a wooden trailer. Sam would look back on that day in conversation with *Scream Magazine*. "Auto Fest is always wild. It's a great show! And we were playing there for the first time. It was our first real gig."

Sam remembered that the band really had it together musically. Those in the audience who were old enough to remember instantly drew the comparison between this band of young kids and early Led Zeppelin. Those who had not yet been born when Led Zeppelin was in full bloom were just digging that their school chums were rocking out. There was promise in the air. There was only one small stumbling block to that first appearance.

"During the course of that show, we had cycled through every song we knew," Sam told *The Detroit News*, "and then all of a sudden we looked at each other and were like 'okay what do we do now?' And all of a sudden, my mom yells out 'play the songs again.'"

Even the more critical in attendance at Auto Fest saw Greta Van Fleet in a promising light. They were young, enthusiastic, very talented and very raw. The consensus was that they might, indeed have a life outside the Frankenmuth city limits.

Shortly after their Auto Fest appearance, drummer Kyle Hauck announced that he was leaving the band. In and of itself, swapping out band members, especially in their early stages, is a fairly common occurrence. A prime example being The Beatles who, on the cusp of superstardom, decided to swap out drummer Pete Best with a ringer named Ringo Starr. It can be a difficult process, rife with battered egos and hurt feelings. Or it can be fairly easy, as offered by the new drummer on the block, Dan, in a conversation with *GratefulWeb.com.* "I replaced the drummer. They said, 'you're better, you play drums.'"

But in fairness to Kyle Hauck, a more detailed explanation only seemed fair. For openers, the oft-cited explanation that Kyle was injured and Dan was a last-minute replacement does not seem to hold water. The reality was that Kyle was of sound body. The reality was that Kyle, two years older than the brothers Kiszka and by all accounts a competent drummer at that stage in the band's development, had his mind set on other things. Dan diagnosed the situation this way in a *Blues Rock Review* interview.

"I think that one of the main reasons behind the replacement was Kyle's age relative to the rest of the guys. It's not that he was too old but the rest of the band was either in middle school or high school and Kyle was getting ready to graduate from high school. Bottom line, he just wasn't sure if music was something he wanted to pursue. It was something where the passion wasn't really there."

And it was something that the rest of the band seemed to sense. Even before the Auto Fest gig, during the garage sessions, Dan was slowly being worked into the starting lineup as a possible replacement. "There was a sense that Kyle might leave the group soon," Dan told *Drum Magazine*, "and so I began to study Kyle's playing. I was practicing just in case he split."

The hunch proved correct as, reportedly mere hours before the band's second official gig, playing an outdoor biker party, Kyle quit the band. The band's parents, with the prospect of a rowdy blowout, most likely including drinking, drugging and guns, would be very much a presence and more-than-capable chaperones at the gig. But what nobody expected was that Greta Van Fleet would have to hunt up a drummer at the last possible moment. Some years later, then-manager Michael Barbee, who had a reputation for shooting from the hip, would give *Alternative Nation.com* a less diplomatic description of Hauck and his departure. "He (Hauck) had some health issues and his work ethic, as a band member, was lacking substantially. He was the kind of guy who wanted to get paid to practice. He let us down. I didn't find out until we were ready to leave for this show at a biker club that he had just hurt his ankle."

Dan told *The Illinois Entertainer* what happened next. "At the time Kyle quit the band, I was playing in an out-of-town golf tournament when I got a call from Sam saying, 'We know you play drums. Would you be able to fill in?' I was so excited. I was two hours away but my dad drove me back to the gig in two hours. The gig was called American Spirit and was put on by a biker club. They had built this huge bonfire out in the woods. It was my first show and it would end up lasting four hours. We were having such a good time playing together that the bikers finally had to turn the generator off to get us to stop playing."

The aftermath of the biker blowout was immediate. The chemistry on stage had improved 100% with Dan behind the drum kit. Jake would later acknowledge that it was the first time he had felt really comfortable onstage. Dan had hopes that the gig would be more than a one-off. But by its conclusion he knew definitely.

"At that point, the torch was officially passed to me."

Greta Van Fleet was now officially a band. It was at that point that they began thinking and acting like one. Dan updated his drum kit through a Craigslist ad and the Papa Kiszka father laid down some red carpet in the garage, effectively transforming the space into a more serious music sanctuary. In a moment of youthful bravado, the members of Greta Van Fleet drafted a primitive contract in which they pledged undying loyalty to each other and allegiance to the musical road ahead.

"Looking back on it, the legalities of that contract were not there," Dan clarified in an interview with *Medleyville.us*. "It was something that made us all feel pretty official and it gave us our responsibilities. We had assigned practice dates in it and it outlined the importance of being at a certain place at a certain time."

Chapter Six

Bikers and Bars

Michael Barbee knew talent when he heard it. And when it came to Greta Van Fleet, the Midwest-based manager had heard quite a bit.

Although reports at the time were a bit sketchy, there is much evidence that Barbee may well have attended a local BBQ and was in the audience at one of the last informal gigs the band performed, a grad party in Frankenmuth. The result was that Barbee's managerial instincts clicked into overdrive. But not at first.

"When I first saw Greta Van Fleet, it was at a BBQ and I didn't really want to go," he remembered in conversation with *Alternative Nation.com*. "But I ended up going. When I got there, I almost left because I saw that it was just a bunch of kids and I felt they didn't know anything about rock 'n' roll. Then they set up and they played the first song. It was a Cream song; I think it might have been "Crossroads." There was something about it. It was so good.

"I knew that they were something special," Barbee recalled in *Redburn Review.com*. "I knew they were a local band but they had the potential to make it to a national stage."

Barbee's background indicates that he was every bit the novice that Greta Van Fleet was. "I had been doing

39

some work out of Detroit with the Reed &Dickinson Band," he related to *Review Magazine.* "It basically boiled down to I'd work if they had any gigs. At that time my ears were wide open. I just wanted to learn management. I'd learned a lot and felt I could take a band like Greta Van Fleet and get them somewhere."

But before he could make his pitch to the band, he had to convince their parents. Given their age and a basic uneasiness about exposing their children to somebody they knew nothing about wanting to manage them, it was understandable that the Kiszka's and the Wagner's were reluctant to turn Greta Van Fleet over to a complete stranger. But as Karen Kiszka recalled during an interview with *The Ladies Of Comedy* podcast, his pitch was, if nothing else, convincing.

"Michael had seen them playing and said, 'Have your parents call me.' So we talked with him and met with him and he said, "This is what's missing. These boys have what's missing in music today. I know a bit and I've been involved in the industry. I would like to help them get to where they are going."

Barbee understood the parents' reluctance to turn their children over to a stranger but he was not dissuaded. Throughout the remainder of 2013, there would be a subtle but consistent courtship. When the band heard about the offer, they were alternately excited and scared. Less than a handful of gigs in and now this kind of attention?

In the meantime, Greta Van Fleet chased any gigs they could find. Word of the success at the American Spirit party got around and soon the band was fielding similar offers from other biker clubs. And so, on those occasions, the band would pack their equipment into the family van or a trailer and would, literally, drive a couple of hours out of town into some deep, dark woods in the middle of nowhere, usually in the middle of the night.

Jake recalled the ritual in conversation with *Classic Rock*. "We'd drive two or three hours north, set up on a small stage or trailer, hook into a generator and play for three or four hours. It was usually around midnight that we would pack up and leave."

For a group of young teens from a small town, Greta Van Fleet had their eyes opened wide as to what it was like playing before a really rough and potentially dangerous crowd during the biker gigs. Sam acknowledged that "sometimes things got violent" and that, on one occasion, an irate audience member nearly hit Dan's father in the face. Throw in incidents of rampant drug and alcohol use, guns being fired in the air and an overall belligerent attitude on the part of the bikers and it was a hardcore introduction to the rock life.

In later years, the members of Greta Van Fleet would often jokingly describe those wild and sometimes scary times in a manner that indicated they may or may not have been joking or prone to youthful exaggeration. For the record, Sam, during *a Grammy Museum* event interview put it this way "Sometimes we would go into bathrooms saying 'Please don't let a drug deal be going down in there. I just want to sit and read Tolkien.'"

"A lot of the stuff we saw at those shows was not normal for kids of our age to be seeing," Jake told *Classic Rock*. "It was kind of scary but the bikers seemed to love us. Once we got up and started playing, there seemed to be some kind of respect between the bikers and the band. If we had been terrible, they probably would have rioted. But we definitely gained respect because of our level of musicianship."

Sam emphasized those biker days when he told *Click On Detroit.com* that their looks did not make those gigs easy. "One of our struggles in the beginning was that nobody really took us seriously. Imagine these four kids with fancy haircuts and these bikers, who are all like 60 or 70 years old, expecting us to be like The Jonas Brothers or something. We'd get up on stage and play rock 'n' roll and that's when we'd earn the biker's respect."

The year 2013 would be a turning point for Greta Van Fleet. After months of persistence, Barbee convinced the Kiszka family that he was on the up and up and he officially became their manager. What sold the band on his services was his concept of slow and steady and word of mouth. It was a time-honored notion that, in the era of *American Idol* and celebrity shortcuts, had fallen into disfavor by those who, quite simply, did not want to work that hard. But it was what Greta Van Fleet was after.

It was also the year that Greta Van Fleet would first venture into a recording studio to lay down some tracks. The studio was Metro 37 in Detroit and local Detroit producer Kevin Sharpe would produce the sessions. Little if anything is known about the particulars of those 2013 sessions except for the fact that they produced what would be the very first recording of "Highway Tune," which would ultimately be pressed as a single and released, more as a promotional offering than anything commercial. It quickly became the first true Greta Van Fleet collectible.

But there was still much to do to get the band up and running. One of the most important was the reality of balancing high school and rock 'n' roll. Josh and Jake were in the home stretch as seniors and had designs on going to college, but Dan and Sam still had a couple years of high school to go, which actually was not too much of a stumbling block as the boys quite naturally evolved a schedule that would allow for both school and gigs. School and practice during the week, gigs on the weekend, and back to school on Monday.

"It isn't easy," Josh told *Review Magazine.com* of the band's balancing act. "It takes more time now. We sleep less. Luckily we can balance school and music. You have to make the decision to be on top of stuff or else it can suck you under and drown you."

With Barbee now working in conjunction with the parents, 2013 would be a gradual roll out of the band with 23 dates, primarily in bars around Michigan, including a total of five performances in Frankenmuth, four in Fischer Hall and one on a Friday Fun Night.

The Frankenmuth shows were relatively easy. Home crowd, familiar surroundings, and an environment where they could do no wrong. The real test would come when the band hit the road where dive bars like The Cork Pine Eatery and Saloon in Vassar; the now-closed New York New York in Chesterfield; and annual The Dirt Fest in Birch Run flew by in a blur of long van rides, late nights, long sets, little if any money and the constant reminders that they were a group of kids who had to show their ID's to get in to venues that often catered to hard-drinking adults.

Dan, in a *Meldeyville.us* conversation, had a good laugh at how the band would have to be carded even though they had no intention of drinking (a common practice in most bars in which underage patrons had their hands marked with the no-alcohol equivalent of a scarlet letter. "I had more than my share of X's written on my hand in dark markers. I'm surprised I don't have permanent scars on my hand."

Sam added his two cents when he regaled *Pollstar.com*

with his stories from the bar days. "Sometimes we had a hard time getting into clubs. On rare occasions, we couldn't even go in until it was time to play and when we finished we'd have to get right out again. Sometimes, it was just a pain in the ass. But most of the time I didn't have to worry about it because I was in the band."

And much like The Beatles in their early Hamburg, Germany days, Greta Van Fleet was having the rock 'n' roll equivalent of on-the-job training. They learned how to pace themselves in a live setting, how to structure a set, how to interact with an audience that, more often than not, would be in various states of drunkenness, and, perhaps most importantly, gradually transformed from a young garage band into a professional-looking and sounding group. The members of Greta Van Fleet were quick learners and would log each gig in that first year in a mental notebook to be accessed in the future.

Sam waxed philosophical about those days with *QRO Magazine*. "There's a difference between someone who wins a television talent show like *The Voice* and someone who has worked their way up playing crappy bars in Saginaw, Michigan. We started out doing the small things, playing for maybe ten people one night and maybe two people the next night. You do the gigs, you gather the experiences, you learn from them and then you move on."

Dan echoed those salad days in a conversation years later with *The Coachella Valley Weekly*. "When we were playing bars, we were just a small band, nothing specific. We were just a local cover band. We would get crazy time slots to play four or five-hour shows. At that point, we were just playing covers but we would often end up with 30 minutes at the end of the night.

"At that point, we would just jam out."

Chapter Seven

One Night at Jan's Bar and Grill

In the annals of Greta Van Fleet lore, Jan's Bar and Grill takes a bow as host of a special moment.

Located in the backwater town of Swartz Creek, Michigan, Jan's, on casual observation, is not that unusual; a haven for beer and happy hour food specials, a hot and sweaty good-time place where people could cut loose, lie back and, occasionally, hear some live music. Jan's Bar and Grill was the first time Greta Van Fleet played live in a bar setting. It was their third show of 2013 following a pair of shakedown shows at Fischer Hall in Frankenmuth. And, according to eyewitness accounts, it was the first time Greta Van Fleet got paid to perform.

Connie King, the owner of Jan's Bar and Grill, and her sons Troy and Shayne Medore, who worked at the bar, spoke to the author in a 2019 interview.

February 2, 2013. This is how it all went down.

"I was running the bar at the time" recalled Shayne, "and was trying to drum up some business. So I put an ad in Craigslist looking for bands. They responded. I didn't realize it at the time that this was their very first gig."

Shayne remembered that the negotiations, conducted through email and Gmail with the band member's father/manager went without a snag. "He (the father) "was real cool. He was easy to deal with."

Connie echoed her son's impression of the dad's sincerity. "The dad came in with the kids. They were quite young, very young. They could not have been much older than 13 or 15. They were nowhere close to drinking age. The dad was insistent that he would be with them at all times and that he would make sure they would not be drinking. He was just looking for somebody to give them a chance and I thought 'why not?'"

Connie and Shayne were convinced. But when it came to Troy, it was a tale of two stories.

Connie said, "My son Troy talked me into letting them play. I said, 'I don't know if we should. They're minors.' But he said, 'No ma, I think we should give them a chance.'" Troy chuckled at the notion that he had convinced her. "Actually, she convinced me. I didn't want a bunch of young kids running around here. I didn't expect anything bad to happen. They were young kids but their parents were around so they weren't going to run around getting into things. But from a pure business side, I was still doubtful. Why would I let a bunch of minors come in here? They weren't going to drink and they weren't going to bring a lot of customers into the place. I wasn't for it. I told my mom, 'Why would you do that? I said no.' But at the end of the day, she's my mom so we agreed to let them play."

The going rate for a band playing Jan's Bar and Grill was $100. It was non-negotiable and the band immediately agreed. It was a moment to remember. It would be their first professional show. "Typically, when I had a band in for a hundred bucks, I'd feel bad and give them free drinks," said Shayne. "Obviously they couldn't drink so my girlfriend made them some chicken to eat.

And why not? They were the nicest bunch of kids. It was all 'please and thank you.'"

Connie remembered that promoting the show was way below grass roots. "Basically it was all word of mouth. We had a sign outside but that probably didn't do a whole lot of good because nobody had really heard of them."

Troy recalled the night of the show when the band arrived early for a sound check. "They showed up in the family car with a trailer for the equipment. There wasn't a tour bus or anything like that."

The performance space that night was reconfigured. Pool tables were moved out of the way to provide a small space for the band near the bar. Connie recalled that, as she watched the members of Greta Van Fleet unload and set up their own equipment and sound check, she was holding her breath. "They came in for the sound check and then had to leave the bar. They couldn't come back in until it was time to play. I was a little bit nervous. All I needed was for a minor to be caught doing something in the bar. But their parents were around them all the time and they didn't even try to drink. They were good."

One hundred people in the bar was considered par for the course when Jan's Bar and Grill had a band in. While nobody would claim that many in the bar when Greta Van Fleet hit the stage, Connie would remember that "the place was full." Troy acknowledged that the audience "was maybe a hundred people."

The band kicked off the first of what would be two sets with "Highway Tune." To this day, Troy recalled getting goose bumps at what he heard. "It was just the vocals at first. Then the band kicked in and it was like holy shit!! My brother and I were sitting at the end of the bar, which is right next to where they played. We looked at each other and just kept saying 'holy shit!' I had no idea who these guys were. It didn't matter that this was just a bar. Nobody had any idea who these guys were. Everybody was just blown away."

Connie conceded that the type of music the band was playing was not really her thing. "But given that, I was definitely impressed with their musicianship and their playing. We had some seasoned local musicians come in that night who told me they were impressed by their skill set for their age. I had thought they would be nothing but they were actually very good. Between sets they hung out and talked to people in the bar. They were really friendly. I think they were ecstatic that they were playing in front of a lot of people and that the people really liked them. To them, our full bar must have seemed like a lot of people. You could tell that they were very happy to be here."

Shayne was so blown away by how well Greta Van Fleet went down that night that he immediately approached the father to have them come back and play again. "He said yes but not for $100. He said, 'I could probably get you a return gig but it was going to cost at least double.' I knew my mom wouldn't go for that. So that was pretty much it."

But the fallout was immediate according to Connie. "People find out that this was the first place they ever played and they flip out. That was what was so cool about it. I would love it if they would come back and play. But they're making too much money now and we can't afford them."

After the show, the band packed up their equipment and drove off into the night, leaving Shayne with the lasting impression that they had been in on the ground floor of something that would be very big. "After that night, we just knew those kids were going to blow up."

Chapter Eight

Living the Life

For all intents and purposes, 2014 would go down as the year Greta Van Fleet began to take themselves seriously, understanding as a band that music would be serious business. The shows the previous year had proven that point. They were definitely still kids but they had taken a giant step forward into the man's game of rock 'n' roll.

Josh and Jake had followed high school graduation by enrolling in college, a fairly disingenuous attempt at higher education that did not last long. Josh would occasionally acknowledge his passion for film and a possible career in cinema and would noted at one point that he had been "interested in maybe going to film school." Jake made no pretense of it being "all music all the time." Sam and Dan still had a ways to go in high school, but the steady encroachment of a life in music had made those last school years a grind. Dan's prowess as a golfer often had him fantasizing about the possibility of turning pro on the links.

For the members of Greta Van Fleet, some hard decisions were being made.

"We kind of did skip over college," Jake told *Phoenix New Times*. "Josh and I did one year of college before we had to sort of reexamine what we'd be doing for this (the music) to take off. I think it would be interesting to go back and have that chapter. But by that time we had already missed a whole lot of chapters."

For better or worse, by 2012 they had already put academics and "normal" teen activities in their rearview mirror in favor of music. Hanging out? Going to movies? Discovering girls? If they weren't writing music, jamming or playing gigs, the normal tropes of adolescence were of no interest.

Jake and Josh, in separate conversations with *The Salt Lake City Tribune* and *Phoenix New Times*, were wistful but matter of fact about the life choices they had been making and, in a sense, making personal sacrifices in favor of their passion for music.

"It was natural to organically come together as a band," reflected Jake. "When the kids in our grade would be hanging out and doing kid stuff, we would be in some dive bar playing every weekend."

Josh echoed those sentiments. "We missed the hanging out on weekends with friends because we were in bars, playing three or four hours on weekends."

Greta Van Fleet continued to crisscross the state of Michigan throughout 2014, marking a milestone of sorts on May 2 when they ventured outside the state for the first time for a show at the Mainstream in Toledo, Ohio. It was a time of creative growth for the band, their performing and songwriting chops maturing at a lightning pace. And the band was beginning to make strides in getting their music out into the public.

With Barbee's guidance, they were becoming a real word-of-mouth juggernaut. A showcase at their Frankenmuth stomping grounds, Fischer Hall, not surprisingly brought out an audience full of local supporters. But the presence of outsiders, musical people from the big city, were also starting to make their presence felt.

Vinnie Dombroski from Detroit-area alt rockers Sponge was spotted at the show having an animated conversation with Barbee, and suggested the band might like working with Al Sutton at Rustbelt Studios. As it turned out, Sutton was also present at the Fischer Hall show and would express his interest to Barbee about the possibility of working with the band. But like everything else swirling around this fledgling group, it was all vague; nothing resembling concrete. For their part, the members of Greta Van Fleet were wide-eyed with excitement as they heard bits and pieces of promising news.

Jake was philosophical when he quipped to *Music Connection*, "We've been pretty dedicated to our craft from the start." Sam offered *Vulture.com* that Greta Van Fleet's bar and biker education stemmed from a notion that playing rock 'n' roll in the backwaters was a journey back to the rock 'n' roll basics. "I think it's all to the roots organic. When we were playing, we put our very heart and soul into the sound. You learn a lot when you play in shitty bars and biker clubs. It really made us develop to play like a band."

In late 2013, Greta Van Fleet took a giant step toward the mainstream when they signed with a Midwest media/licensing company called North Star Media as an outlet for getting their songs licensed for commercial, television and other media. By now officially installed as the band's manager, Michael Barbee was proving a down-to-earth, instinctive self-starter, especially when it came to getting the word out on his charges. "We gave them the music," Barbee told *MLive.com* of his decision to take the band's songs to North Star Media. "We kind of wanted them to shop it around."

When speaking with *Review Magazine.com,* Barbee would further acknowledge the vibe within the band when North Star Media took them on: "We were all into the band signing that publishing deal. Everybody knew that was going to get the music out there and we were pretty excited about that."

North Star Media, fully ahead of the curve, liked what they heard of this totally unknown band and began marketing the GVF's music. They found a willing customer in a regional Detroit auto dealership looking for some driving music to goose an ad for their line of Chevy cars, the Equinox. Consequently, by early 2014, the very first Greta Van Fleet song, "Standing On," would appear for a time as the backdrop for the sleek auto brand. The 30-second commercial presented a middle-class, middle American family cruising happily along life's highway on their way to fun in the snow and on the slopes while Greta Van Fleet's music spurs them to put their SUV in a higher gear. Truth be told, the ad was typical corporate advertising. But the band's music made it something not only tolerable but downright special.

That same year, the band would make the rather unconventional decision, even for the time, to create a crowdfunding effort that would ultimately result in a one day, one session, no takes session of a live EP entitled *Greta Van Fleet: Live in Detroit.* It was recorded at Groove Box Studios and ultimately released in limited numbers on the Pledge Music label.

The EP contained early band originals "Highway Tune," "Cloud Train," "Lover Leaver Taker Believer,"

"Standing On" and "Written In Gold." Not surprisingly, *Live in Detroit* was a rough, raw collection. But the quality of the performance and the obvious level of talent for a group not yet out of their teens could not be denied.

The band looked at the experience as part of their growing process, dealing with being in a studio and the pressures of basically having one shot at it. But, as Jake explained in *Gulf Times*, the big deal about making *Live in Detroit* was more sentimental than anything else. "It was our family, friends and fans that gave us the money," he said. "We were lucky to have a fan base even back in those days. They believed in us and what we were doing. We had never seen such devoted people."

Chapter Nine

The Rustbelt Follies

By 2015, Greta Van Fleet had a stranglehold on the state of Michigan. Two years of non-stop touring within the state had brought them a degree of recognition and the first rush of media interest outside the state. Now they were poised to take the next step.

"We wrote a bunch of songs a while ago," Jake related to *Guitar World*. "But when we started thinking about recording we realized, 'Hey, we can do better than this.' "We were more and more seasoned from touring. There's something about consistently playing before a live audience that just forces you to grow. At that point, I think we were all pretty unanimous about what we needed to do."

Under Barbee's steady hand, Greta Van Fleet chose to cut back on touring. Point of fact: The comprehensive *Setlist.com* listed only three shows during 2015, one each in the months of May, June and October. The rest of the time was spent in relative seclusion, writing new material and working their way through a series of regional recording studios, creating demos and sifting through the possibilities of where and who might be a good fit to record their first album.

"I think we wanted to find someone in a place that could better our approach to what we wanted to do and what sound we wanted to get," Jake told *Guitar World*. Looking for the right studio quickly narrowed down their choices to a pair of well-respected Detroit-area recording studios, Metro 37 and Plymouth Rock Recording Co. In the case of Metro 37, there was a sense of familiarity, having worked with that outlet's producer Kevin Sharpe on earlier recording projects.

Greta Van Fleet was taking the selection of a recording studio more seriously than most. Rather than selecting any competent studio and producer to put together an album in order to catch the ear of a record label and not worrying about setting a vibe that would mesh with theirs, the band was taking their time, looking for a perfect marriage of style and substance.

Being in a studio environment would prove a creative shot in the arm. Away from the logistics of traveling and performing, the members of Greta Van Fleet were seemingly pushed inward, and the result was a large number of new songs, often created literally from scratch while the band fashioned demo tapes.

Josh related to *I'm Music Magazine* how one such session at Plymouth Rock resulted in the creation of one of their best-known tunes, "Safari Song." "We were doing some writing and recording at Plymouth Rock. At one point, we were playing a bunch of old blues songs and Jake came up with this riff that I fell in love with. It had this sense of complexity, the mixture of jungle music and the blues and it made me think of a jungle safari, hence the title "Safari Song." The lyrics to the song were written as a narrative, the way many blues songs have been written."

The metamorphosis of Greta Van Fleet was now in

full flower. Some may have taken the demands, probing questions and opinions exhibited during those early studio sessions by the group as youthful ego. Ultimately their confidence in knowing what they wanted to do musically would be the driving factor in finding those early studio sessions often less than satisfying.

"We had two studio experiences," Sam offered in *Glide Magazine* and, some years later in *The Pop Bank.com*, "But the problem was that the producers weren't really putting in their point of view and that's the most important thing a producer can have is a point of view and to make the music sound good. We had recording experience but it was more like an assembly line. We would come in and put the drums down, the bass down, the guitars and vocals and then mess around with it for a little bit."

Jake added to the critique of the previous studio experiences with *Loudwire.com*. Ever the diplomat, the guitarist refused to name names and cite specific instances but, rather, painted an overall picture of the experience. "We'd been in a couple of studios with the idea of maintaining our own thing. You see people getting into situations and people always ending up yelling at the producers and engineers about 'let's keep it this way or something.'"

But being budding perfectionists, nothing seemed to rub them the right way, and so the search continued.

Al Sutton of Michigan-based Rustbelt Studios had been in the music business for more than 25 years. His credits included work with Kid Rock, Hank Williams Jr., Lynyrd Skynyrd, ZZ Top, Sheryl Crow and countless others. He has seen and heard it all and was not easily impressed. But when he'd caught the band during the previous Frankenmuth show, he sensed something special, so he was receptive to a call from Barbee the following year.

"In the Spring of 2015, we got a call from the band's manager," Sutton recalled in a *Sound On Sound* interview. "He asked us if we'd be willing to record this band he had called Greta Van Fleet. The demos they sent looked promising. When they came in and I heard them I was just blown away."

Sutton's partner, Marlon Young, was a straightforward, no-bullshit kind of guy. His assessment upon meeting and listening to the band was both enlightening and on the mark, as evidenced in a quote from *Rock Bands Of Los Angeles.com*. "There's a young band called Greta Van Fleet from Frankenmuth, that place up past Flint where all the chickens come from. They're these little kids that have this big Zeppelin influence and are really into it. I'm not sure what their end game is but it's obvious that the first and foremost thing is not 'We gotta be famous.' It's refreshing."

For their part, the band conceded that they were literal babes in the woods when they walked into Rustbelt Studios for the first time. "We knew nothing about the studio," Jake admitted to *The Detroit Free Press*. "We weren't studio musicians. We weren't familiar with that side of the world."

Nor were they really focused on the idea of the studio as an important role in their rock 'n' roll life as Josh told *The Detroit Free Press*. "There was no real goal for us at that point. We were just looking for the experience. All we wanted to do was to track some of our stuff."

Given their inexperience, Greta Van Fleet had seemingly stumbled onto the ideal mentor. Sutton could be encouraging or critical in a subtle manner, knowing full well that talented but youthful musicians needed kid gloves when it came to their music. As he had already proved several times over with major acts, he was instinctive when it came to the basic principles of recording, the best way to approach an idea and how to get certain sounds. And in the case of Greta Van Fleet, it meant diving deeper, well beyond the popular conceit that the band was nothing more than a Led Zeppelin clone.

"Al Sutton saw something in us which was incredible," Sam told *The 405*, "Because we weren't a proper band at that point and he was the guy who said these guys have something." Dan hinted at Sutton's sense of tough love when it came to the band in the same *405* article. "He never really told us that we had 'it.' He never put it to us that way. He said these guys have potential. They don't have 'it' but they have potential."

The chemistry between producer and band was seemingly instantaneous. Sutton was so excited by Greta Van Fleet's potential that he immediately called up his partner, producer Young and exclaimed, "You've got to hear these kids." Sutton and Young agreed that the possibilities for greatness and rock stardom were definitely in place. Now it was just a matter of making their young charges wiser in the way of recording, which even the band had to admit, was an alien concept.

Sam explained their naiveté to *Out Of The Box.com*. "When we set foot in that studio for the first time, we didn't know anything about how to make an actual recording. We kind of knew what the process entailed. But once we hooked up with Al we began to learn a lot."

And the first thing they learned was that in Al Sutton, they had a not-too-subtle taskmaster. "Al is a great producer because he isn't going to lie to you," Sam reflected in *The Pop Breaks.com*. "He's going to tell you the truth and tell you exactly how it is. Al is Al. We knew we would learn a lot from him just by his being point blank. He would say things like 'That's a shitty part. Okay, let's rethink it and take it in a different direction.'"

Chapter Ten

Knowledge and Practice Breeds Evolution

Midway through 2015, Greta Van Fleet made the decision to come off the road, the better to spend their lives for the next two years at Rustbelt Studios, learning to translate their already potent live show into equally effective vinyl.

There was also that little matter of Sam and Dan being seniors in high school, some months away from graduation, to consider. The two younger members had already relegated high school life to the back burner but, either in deference to their parents' wishes that they get a diploma, or to have a last official fling with their friends from school, Sam and Dan were diligent in doing right by the formalities of their high school education, burning the candle at both ends. They made sure homework was done correctly and on time, maintained good grades, this allowing time to get to the studio. Dan acknowledged the balancing act in conversation with *The Illinois Entertainer*. "Sam and I were just finishing up high school. There were a lot of days where I would do my homework and then go to the studio."

According to *Setlist.com*, the only live show the band would play through the end of 2016 would be on the bill of Freakfest in Saginaw, Michigan. The band was philosophical about the idea of spending their time writing and recording under the tutelage of Sutton and Young, deeming it a necessary and positive next step.

Sam explained it this way during a *Grammy Museum* event interview. "Knowledge and practice breeds evolution. We needed the time to mature."

And as Jake would recall in *Loudwire.com*, the producers at Rustbelt were exactly what the band needed. "It was a very steep learning curve. I would like to say that, now, we're a bit more seasoned. For us, there was so much insight that they brought to the table."

But while the band was hunkered down in their creative bunker, they were never far from the growing outside acknowledgement of their existence. By the first of the year, the agreement between Greta Van Fleet and North Star Media had expired and was not renewed. However, as a final parting gift to the band, North Star Media had negotiated one more bit of business, the insertion of the song "Highway Tune" into episode two, season six of the Showtime television series *Shameless,* a deal that was finalized while Greta Van Fleet was still a North Star Media client.

It was also around that time and, perhaps due to the over-enthusiastic comments by both band and manager, that speculation was floated that no less a light than Bob Seger and Kid Rock producer Edward "Punch" Andrews had taken an extreme liking to the band and that he would be, according to an *Mlive.com* report, be producing a five-song EP that would be released in either April or May of 2016. "Originally we were going to do a five song EP," Barbee reported. "He (Andrews) is kind of leading the way at this point." But like so many stories floated every day in the music industry, the Andrews-produced EP proved to be just smoke and mirrors.

The reality was that while the band was a bit premature in predicting a release date, Greta Van Fleet had been working at a lightning pace since falling in with Sutton and Young and, along the way, singer/producer Herschel Boone since in late 2015. The collective and often laidback approach to getting the best out of their young charges at Rustbelt had an immediate and desired effect on the band.

Josh recalled with no small bit of pride to *Sing Me A Story.com* that "We had written and recorded 20 songs (during that period). We had so many songs that we were working on it was ridiculous. But the bottom line is that we're just trying to develop and get better. That's very important to us."

And the creative rush the band was feeling was not limited to the four walls of Rustbelt. With the first signs of claustrophobia setting in, the band decided they needed a break and some fresh air. Jake recalled that "break" from the studio in *The Red And Black.com*. "We went down to Chattanooga where we rented a cabin for a week and still ended up writing five new songs. Everything's been going very quickly."

Sutton acknowledged that he had seen and heard just about everything in his years in the music business but even he had to admit, in a *Mixonline.com* interview, that the members of Greta Van Fleet had an intensity and drive that was a first for him. "They're not excited by 12-hour days," Sutton offered. "We'll be working here, messing around with something, and look up and all of a sudden they're gone. We would find them out in the lobby, the four of them with acoustic guitars, just jamming for hours on end. They're in a constant jam session. They don't want to just sit there and do it. They want to be out there playing and singing. They never stop playing. It's just fascinating to watch."

Over the months in the studio, the transformation of the band into a lineup that could effectively translate their already potent live sound to vinyl continued.

A lot of technical issues became a part of the repertoire along with such seemingly minor issues as the placing of the instruments in the studio for that maximum live feel. For Sutton, Young and Boone the challenges were often on a par with those of the band. But, bottom line, Greta Van Fleet's education was on their terms. In a *Sound On Sound.com* article, Young was duly impressed with the band's determination to do things their way. "When the band started with us, there were immediately people who said, 'What you do is a little Led Zeppelin, perhaps you need to change that.' But the band said 'We're not here to play some music industry game. We're not changing anything.' "

Midway through 2016, Greta Van Fleet arrived at a serious next step. Press for the still relatively unknown band had been good and the group was continuing to cultivate a group of 'heavy friends' in the industry. It was time to put a presentable package together for prospective labels. An EP seemed the ideal solution, something that would showcase both their music and songwriting skills as well as their studio savvy.

"We already had quite a repertoire of songs to draw from," Josh told *Metal Riot.com*. "So we handpicked four songs that we felt would fit together, that would be a cohesive collection and that would give the EP an overall sound."

The songs selected were their signature song, "Highway Tune", "Safari Song", "Flower Power" and "Black

Smoke Rising." The choices adhered largely to their Zeppelin/British Invasion influences. But Dan, talking up the EP to *The Prelude Press.com*, cited an evolution for the band within those four songs. "Three of the four songs were written three years ago. I look at those songs as being our 'youthful stage.' "Black Smoke Rising" was written in the last year. I'd like people to look at these songs and be able to see our development. For me, there is such a huge difference energetically and spiritually between "Highway Tune" and "Black Smoke Rising."

With Sutton, Young and Boone at the controls, Greta Van Fleet turned out all four songs in three days. It would be three days in which the members of the band proved their maturity in a studio setting while reinforcing their talents at projecting a sound that was both new and old. Young was beside himself with admiration for his young charges when discussing the band sometime after that pivotal recording session with *Mixonline.com*. "It's like they stepped out of 1976. The entire mentality to the music, the reason they do it, what they feel it stands for, the sounds they like. It's not even that they're trying to do it. It's just who they are."

For the band, completing the EP which would ultimately be christened *Black Smoke Rising*, it was a time to celebrate, a time when they could bask in a job well done and a true musical representation of what they do best. Sam was particularly thrilled, telling *Screamer Magazine*...

"I wanted the EP to come out the very next day."

Sam's youthful enthusiasm aside, the band, while stoked on their accomplishment, was basically ho-hum about this next step in their evolution as a band. "There was no goal at that point," Jake offered in interviews with

The Detroit Free Press and *Blabbermouth.net*. "We were just looking for the experience. We weren't looking to put out an album or anything. "I don't think we ever planned to be on any label because of the approach and the type of music we play. We wanted to build it up from the bottom and do it on our own."

Chapter Eleven

Sign Here Please

Marlon Young knew people, and it was not only the working stiffs in the rock 'n' roll trenches.

He knew people on the business side of the music industry. The dollars-and-cents bottom-line guys who could quantify the success potential of raw, creative talent; people who had the know-how to market said talent to the masses. And the buzz following the completion of Greta Van Fleet's four-song demo/EP suddenly had expectations and potential so great that Young was going through his Rolodex, checking under M for management.

Suddenly, Barbee's tenure as the group's manager was looking tenuous. Especially after Young contacted a long-time attorney named Aaron Frank, who worked out of the family business ABI Management, and sent him a copy of the band's material. Frank was thrilled with what he heard. An old rock 'n' roller at heart, his instincts as a fan as well as a businessman were much in evidence. Greta Van Fleet was something he could work with.

For Barbee, the handwriting had already been on the wall for some time. He'd long had a reputation as an anti-establishment type who had been quick to distrust record companies, and had warned the band of his feelings early on. His attitude had worked during those early years on the road. But superstardom on a much higher plateau would necessitate a different skill set and attitude.

"It was about two weeks after we had finished in the studio and it was being talked about that the band needed a manager with more connections than I had," Barbee told *Alternative Nation.com*. "So I reluctantly handed it off to Aaron Frank at ABI Management."

By all accounts, the band was neutral on the subject of changing managers. They would be quick to mention Barbee, often in a laundry list of thank you's, and often not by name. But they had developed a real relationship with Barbee, and when it was suggested that he could stay on as the band's tour manager, Barbee accepted what many, right or wrong, assumed was a consolation prize.

As it turned out, ABI did indeed know all the right people. It was not long after Aaron Frank was bowled over by Greta Van Fleet's ability to effectively transform their impressive live sound to vinyl, as well as their remarkable youth that Frank was on the horn to Jason Flom, the head of Lava Records. He sent Flom a missive and link to the songs "Highway Tune," "Safari Song" and "Flower Power."

Jason Flom had always been a go-with-your-gut kind of guy.

He would listen to just about anything that came across his desk. It didn't matter if it was blatantly commercial or something fringe or contrary. If he liked what he heard, a yay or nay decision would be quickly forthcoming. And it went without saying that his decisions always came from a creative soul. Flom's "ear" led him to sign a seemingly endless string of superstar talent, first with Atlantic Records and, in the mid-'90s, the founding of Lava Records, which would produce hits and stars as diverse as Katy Perry, Kid Rock, Lorde and Jessie J. And it was in a scenario typical of Flom's past decision-making that he would cross paths with Greta Van Fleet.

Flom had a good memory for important dates and his first contact with Greta Van Fleet was no exception. November 11, 2016. 4:43 p.m. Ever the stickler for detail, Flom told *Classic Rock* exactly how it went down.

"I remember I was sitting with my son and I put on "Highway Tune" and I was like 'What the hell is this? This is insane.' I hadn't heard that sound since back in the day. It was an instant reaction. A number of things grabbed me. First it was Josh's voice. It wasn't from a different era but from a different planet. There was something about the way they created music, which I realized was because they had been playing together. And then there was the fact that they were so young. These guys were kids. They were still in high school."

Four days after Flom received the email, the band received a message from their management saying that Jason Flom from Lava Records wanted to sign the band. Needless to say, the band members incredulous, quoted by bystanders as uttering "Bullshit!" upon hearing the news. But Greta Van Fleet was quickly convinced that the offer was real. Plans were formulated for the band to fly to New York and showcase live for Flom. But as Jake related in *Phoenix New Times*, Flom had other ideas. "We went ahead and scheduled a showcase but Flom called and said, 'They don't need to play for me. I'm just gonna sign them.'"

Josh related the band's reaction to being signed to *Billboard.* He knew enough about the way the business worked to realize that this sort of thing did not happen very often. "I'm not sure what sold him (Flom). He must have heard something that I hope had a genuineness to it, a power, a cohesiveness. I really don't know but I'm glad he did."

The next few months were a whirlwind of activity. The concept of booking agents, publicists, entertainment lawyers and marketing experts on a much grander scale than they could ever have imagined were brought before the wide-eyed band and thoroughly explained in minute detail. There was no racing through the fine print; there was patience. Jake recalled on *Blabbermouth.net* that it all boiled down to one defining moment.

"We had a Facechat with Jason. He just wanted to sign us. He was great and the deal was great. So we said okay."

There was only one legal hurdle. All the members of the band had to be 18 to legally sign a contract, and Dan and Sam still had some months to go before they reached the magic number. And so, for the next few months, the band operated under a self-imposed cone of silence, keeping the fact that they were about to sign a major label deal under wraps from all except for their families. And, from their perspective, the decision made perfect sense. In a small town like Frankenmuth, any news traveled fast.

"We didn't tell anybody about the record deal until Sam and I graduated from high school," Dan told *The Illinois Entertainer*. "It was kind of a secret between us. We didn't want a bunch of rumors going around. We come from a town where things can spread very quickly."

By March 2017, everybody in Greta Van Fleet were officially legal. The members happily signed on the bottom line. Now it could be told.

Chapter Twelve

Devil's in the Details

Greta Van Fleet's signatures on the official contract made the whole process legal and binding. The bubbly had been passed around and it was all good cheer. It was at that point that the train, in a business sense, left the station. The negotiations and legalese came together without complications. There was a lot of innate trust on the part of the band members. Truth be known, they had only an inkling about the fine print and the stacks of paper they needed to sign or initial. But in the end, with no small amount of family and lawyer input, they were satisfied.

As reported by *Music Connection* and a whole lot of music media with a business bent, the contract with Lava Records was for five albums, a fairly generous but not-unheard-of commitment to a new band that a label had a whole lot of confidence in. And to hear the 'happy talk" pouring forth in the wake of the signing, it appeared that everybody was on board.

In a *Wall Street Journal* article on the business side of the resurgence of hard rock as commodity, Lava Records CEO Flom enthused, "They're a band with a retro sound, youthful energy and good looks. They appeal to classic rock dads who tune into classic rock radio and attended classic rock concerts, younger male fans curious about the '60s and the '70s and young women who have traditionally helped rock bands become pop stars. They've got the chops, the swagger and the songs."

Almost immediately after signing with Lava, and with the continued guidance of ABI Management, Greta Van Fleet came under the wing of legendary William Morris Agency's music division, Endeavor, and division head Marc Geiger, who immediately gave four agents the task of making Greta Van Fleet a household name. "My hair stood on end the first time I heard this band. They've got so much power, artistry and they can write songs. I truly believe that they can change rock and can become a leading light in the music industry for the next 30 or 40 years."

There's nothing wrong with being positive and upbeat. In the early stages of any kind of business relationship it's always that way. But as it would turn out, the business side of Greta Van Fleet's team was pragmatic and experienced in the way of marketing popular music, be it hard rock or radio-friendly pop. And when it came to Greta Van Fleet, the dots were already being connected so that the band would not wind up being pigeonholed.

"If a rock band like Greta Van Fleet is going to break in this day and age, they have to be positioned differently, not just in the rock world," Geiger told *Pollstar.com*. "How we book them, where we put them, what festivals we choose, who we choose to play in between, which promoters we choose, which clubs we play. It all has to do with keeping the band in today's zeitgeist."

One advantage Greta Van Fleet would have in entering this brave new world is that the band was already in huge demand thanks to endless touring. But from the outset, the suits were smart enough to not skip any steps in the next phase of the band's odyssey, as Geiger offered to Pollstar.com.

"The truth is Greta Van Fleet is capable of selling 100 to 500 percent more tickets than we are allowing them to play. Our team knows that the band's current rate of growth is unnatural for a band that is still growing. Controlling the growth and making sure there is no 'pop' from overexposure is a challenge for us." Geiger elaborated on that element of the band's development in a *Wall Street Journal* piece. "Having them play smaller venues even though we could easily get them booked into bigger venues is part of our vision for the growth of the band. You need to give people this image of 'I saw them at The Troubadour.'"

But the bottom line to this deal was the fact that Greta Van Fleet was not signing away their creative souls. When it came to the music, it was all on them and they were free to do with it what they wanted. And as their manager Aaron Frank so succinctly put it, who could argue with that?

"When you watch them play live, they are communicating without talking. They are all in perfect synch with each other and are communicating, sometimes with a look, sometimes without even looking at each other. They just know what each other is thinking."

Chapter Thirteen

Black Smoke Rising

Their signatures were barely dry on the deal papers before Greta Van Fleet were back in the studio. Because the band was now part of a major label grand plan, getting the band back on the road after a fairly long hiatus was uppermost on everybody's agenda. Right up there with getting an album out as quickly as possible.

The ideal first strike would be a four-song EP entitled *Black Smoke Rising,* with a lightspeed release date of April 2017. What made the process fairly easy was that the quality of the four song-EP/demo recorded in three days in 2016 was, for all intents and purposes, the album that would be released. The songs were vintage Van Fleet, spanning their earliest songwriting efforts and long-favored live songs "Highway Tune," "Safari Song," "Flower Power" and the lesser-known title track "Black Smoke Rising". It was also an album that would play to both the band's strengths and continue to make them a critical target for those continuing to throw the "Led Zeppelin impersonators" tag in their faces.

But the brickbats, and even the laudatory reviews that heavily referenced *Led Zeppelin I* and *II c*uts were not unexpected. The band members continued to readily agree with the reality that the Zeppelin influence was undeniable, as was the blues, '60s and '70 s heavy rock and metal and, as they were often prone to mentioning for shock value, John Denver. But they saw the impending release of *Black Smoke Rising* as important evidence that they were continuing to work hard to expand upon what supporters and detractors alike viewed as obvious.

"*Black Smoke Rising* was a way to test the waters and to get our first piece of work out there," Dan told *BTR Today.com*. "It definitely is an introduction into who we are right now."

Sam echoed that sentiment before hinting in *Glide Magazine* that *Black Smoke Rising* might well be the first of a trilogy of discs that would trace the evolution of Greta Van Fleet from its inception to the here and now. "*Black Smoke Rising* is a connected piece. It's a continuation. It's like telling a story first, then the middle part and then another part."

Black Smoke Rising would prove a particularly nostalgic moment for Jake, as it marked the end of a long journey for his first writing effort "Highway Tune." "The riff to "Highway Tune"" was one of the first riffs I'd ever written," he reminisced to *Loudwire.com*. "I'd written that riff about seven years ago. I brought it to the table about five years ago with the first lineup, and when Dan joined the band, we formatted it. We recorded it at Metro 37, demoed it once, demoed it again at Rustbelt Studios, recorded it there, and that is the version that ended up on *Black Smoke Rising*. That song has been through quite a journey."

Likewise, Sam also indicted in *Glide Magazine* that "Safari Song" went through a bit of evolution from its inception to completion. "Originally the song had a big percussion break in the middle with bongos and congas. It had a very Santana, South American style to it. But that version got cut from the final EP."

The days leading up to the release of *Black Smoke Rising* went by with blinding speed and anticipation. Greta Van Fleet now had a lot of people at their beck and call who were working 24/7 to guide them through the process of endless round of press interviews and marketing work to prime the pump for the album's release. It was to the band's credit that the attitude of Greta Van Fleet as family had readily adjusted to the process.

Everybody had their moments in the interview chair, sometimes as a group, sometimes singularly. In hindsight that strategy seemed designed to keep these still wet-behind-the-ears media novices from getting dizzy due to the rush of interest. The story was the story, and since the band was still a relatively unknown quantity, the story would have to be told through hours on the press trail when the same questions would be repeated endlessly and the celebrity media, at some point, would begin to blend into a blur. It helped that during the earliest press interviews, the group members came across as insightful, entertaining and more than willing to please.

It was all coming quick and fast. And Greta Van Fleet, youthful enthusiasm intact, was ready to take on whatever would come next.

The official rollout of the album would begin on March 31 when iTunes released "Highway Tune" as the band's first official single. On April 18, the accompanying video for "Highway Tune" was released on *Loudwire*. Three days later, April 21, *Black Smoke Rising* had its official unveiling. And the critical response was immediate.

The Cleveland Plain Dealer reported, "Great songs and playing and singer Josh Kiszka has one of the high flying muscular voices that makes rock and roll great." *Screamer* enthused, 'Given how mind blowing, crazy, scary unbelievably good the four songs are, what's even more inspiring is that this is just the first from Greta Van Fleet." *Decibel Geek.com* got into the spirit of things when it brashly intoned, 'These young assholes from Michigan should probably piss you off for being so good and so young."

Good or bad—and to be honest, the reviews would be overwhelmingly positive—the critical eyes had one thing in common. The comparisons between Greta Van Fleet and Led Zeppelin were immediate and hellbent on stating the obvious. To be fair, some of the more observant also gave passing credit to such British Invasion stalwarts as Clapton, Townshend and American blues legend Howlin' Wolf. But for the most part, it was all Zeppelin all the time.

But one thing the band had learned was patience in dealing with the question that had quickly eclipsed the "origin of the band name" queries. So they responded by talking smart, admitting to the Zeppelin influence, but insisting that it was just a springboard that would evolve into a wider creative influence.

However, even at this stage in the band's development, it was beginning to try their collective patience. A couple of years after the release of *Black Smoke Rising*, Josh, in a thinly disguised fit of pique in conversation with *Rolling Stone*, did his best to lay Led Zeppelin to rest. "Obviously we hear the similarity. That's one of the influences of ours. But at this point we've acknowledged it. Let's move on."

Bottom line, *Black Smoke Rising* may have struck many as being a copycat offering but, at a time when real rock was making a comeback and was also hard to find, it didn't make a whole lot of difference. The album was well produced, the band's musical and vocal chops were first rate, and nobody could argue with the quality of the songs, especially as written by teens barely out of high school.

The result was that *Black Smoke Rising* would make a mad dash up the charts. The album would rise to a respectable No. 182 on the *Billboard* Top 200 Album Charts but, as expected, would do even better on the hard rock-specific listings, landing at No. 10 on *Billboard's* Top Hard Rock Album listings and No. 30 on that same publication's US Top Rock Album charts. Albums, both digital and physical, were selling at a brisk clip and, in slightly less than a year would sell an estimated 70,000 copies in the US alone.

Not surprisingly, "Highway Tune" was getting the lion's share of attention and the huge amount of praise for that song was unexpected. "I'm surprised that "Highway Tune" has taken off," Josh offered to *Billboard*. "I had no idea as to what kind of momentum would shroud the whole thing. It garnered attention faster than anyone thought it would. I don't know why people are connecting to it. But the appreciation is surreal and humbling."

Greta Van Fleet were thrilled with the response of *Black Smoke Rising*. But after a short period of high fives, they had other things to consider. It was time to pack their bags and head out on the road for the first time in nearly two years. And all indications were that this tour was going to be a mother.

Chapter Fourteen

On The Job Training

At first look, the logistics of Greta Van Fleet's first major tour since signing with Lava Records were staggering.

A total of 78 dates spread out over eight months would ultimately turn out to be a manageable tour designed to let the band get their sea legs. A series of shows opening for British rockers The Struts was followed by some less-pressure slots on big festivals and concerts before moving up to headlining shows. It seemed the way to allow the band to shake off the performing rust and introduce audiences to the songs from *Black Smoke Rising* and an already written backlog of an additional 25 tunes.

Josh explained to *Loudwire.com* that he liked the idea of moving heretofore unknown songs in and out of their set lists. "Each of our songs has its own gravity and we're really excited for people to hear the diversity of more than just the four songs that have been released."

The announcement of the 2017 tour brought about almost a Beatles-level response. Ten of the first 15 shows sold out in less than two minutes. Not surprisingly, much of the heat continued to result from the unsuspecting rally of *Black Smoke Rising* and the single "Highway Tune," with the latter riding atop the influential Active and Mainstream Rock Radio listing for four weeks, while the accompanying video rang up 2.7 million views on YouTube and 5.2 million Spotify plays. The EP was no slouch either, rising to No. 6 on the Active and Mainstream Rock Radio list while chalking up more than 1.4 million YouTube views in record time. This was all before the first gig. It was no surprise that when the band members tried to deal with this massive success, they were often at a loss for words.

"I think we're handling it pretty well," Jake told *Review Magazine*. "We were all raised right and are caught up in the middle of it. It's kind of hard to sort out where everything is at. It (success) is something you can never really prepare for."

The tour kicked off on May 12 at Austin's Fuel Room in Libertyville, Illinois. In a seemingly smart business move, Greta Van Fleet was tabbed as the opening act for British glam rockers The Struts for six shows. The Struts were older and more experienced musicians who had been slowly slipping into the US rock market. For Greta Van Fleet it would be on-the-job training on a number of fronts, learning the ins and outs of being on the road, playing to larger audiences by degrees and hanging with musicians who had been around a while and had seen quite a bit. Greta Van Fleet's management was proving to be smart that way.

Greta Van Fleet's first live performance of 2017 lasted 30 minutes, just enough time to play *Black Smoke Rising* in its entirety. But it was just enough time to establish that Greta Van Fleet were professional, first-rate heavy rock musicians. The band saw it as a good omen when, at the conclusion of their set, an appreciative audience quite literally would not let them leave.

"One of the most amazing things that happened would have to be the reception we garnered from audiences and this happened at all of the six shows we did with The Struts," Jake told *Alternative Nation.* "When we would finish our set and walk off stage the crowd continued to cheer. We'd wait about five minutes for them to stop but they continued to applaud and cheer. We didn't have roadies at that time and so we had to go back on stage and pack up our own gear. The crowds continued to cheer while we packed up. That was certainly nothing we had anticipated."

Years later, the memories of those first shows would come back to Jake during an interview with *HM Magazine.* "I didn't expect that we would be getting so little sleep. We were either on the road, in the van, at the venue or at the hotel. It was tiring and exhilarating and we just got to get up on stage and make our music. It was insane."

During those early gigs, the members of Greta Van Fleet also learned some seemingly minute but ultimately important lessons about living the rock 'n' roll life. And as Sam sheepishly explained to *Alternative Nation*, one of the most important was: don't lose your instruments.

"After the first show with The Struts we were packing up to leave. I remember looking around to make sure I had everything and then we took off. It wasn't until we arrived at the next gig that I realized that I had forgotten one of my basses and it wasn't even mine. Marlon Young, one of our co-producers, had lent it to me for the tour. You can imagine how awful I felt and I had no idea how I was going to make it right. When we got to the gig, I walked in and there, propped up in the middle of the floor, was Marlon's bass with a note attached to it that read 'Free to a good home. My owner left me behind.' It turned out that The Struts had found it when they were packing up and brought it with them."

Over the course of those six shows, the band grew to be good mates with The Struts and, in the process, overcame the question of compatibility that had been haunting them since those first shows were announced.

"We had some questions," Josh admitted to *Billboard*. "Is this the right match for us? Can we do anything with it? Can we make music with other people? What we found out was that they (The Struts) were tight and genuinely good people. It was a lot of fun doing that. This was perfect."

The first five months of the tour flew by in a blur of sights, sounds and places the band was seeing for the first time. In fact, every gig was a new experience where Greta Van Fleet got up close and personal with the rock 'n' roll life.

Having a big-time label and top-notch management meant there were more people to tell them what to do, where and when to be someplace, and who to talk to. Some things did not change. They were still playing gigs where they were not old enough to drink, although band members were, outside of the occasional beer, teetotalers. The long hours leading up to sound checks and then the actual performance often found the band members strumming acoustics in some quiet corner, jamming or playing around with new ideas and songs. Depending on the situation, the end of a show often found Greta Van Fleet in the crowd, engaging the audience in lively conversations.

The group was seemingly in a constant state of mental and physical exhaustion. They quickly found that sleep was often at a premium and often a luxury between press interviews. That dues-paying for up-and-coming bands, the endless long drives into cities large, small and miniscule scattered coast to coast and into the heartland would be a true test of their chemistry. Little sleep and close proximity has killed more than one rock 'n' roll career. But as Jake told *Pollstar.com*, that was not a problem.

"Traveling around in a van is not all that bad. We really get along with each other which is good because sometimes we have 12 hour drives that we do in one night."

June and July saw the band crisscrossing Wisconsin and Michigan for slots in the Shake The Lake Festival, The National Cherry Festival and Summerfest before hitting the club circuit with occasional forays into the big city, including gigs at Hollywood's notorious Viper Room and east coast shows, in particular, New York City.

Although they would dismiss the idea that some gigs were more important than others, they could not get away from the reality—or perception—that fans on the coasts tended to be more hip, sophisticated and could be a tougher crowd for a new band. Jake would admit as much to *Review Magazine* when he said "The Viper Room and the New York shows, those were kind of defining moments for us. We wanted to show those audiences that we were ready. But wherever we go, everybody attending our shows is glad to be there to rock and roll."

In the grand tradition of rock 'n' roll immemorial, Greta Van Fleet was on a very long, strange trip. But at the end of the day, at the show, there was always the carrot of primal acceptance.

"Sure, it was a long, hard, exhausting experience,"

Jake reflected of that first tour to *Billboard*. "But at the end there was always the grandeur of being able to play in front of people who were there to see you."

And as the tour continued, it was obvious that the band's post doctorate at rock 'n' roll university was having the desired effect. With each passing show Greta Van Fleet was becoming more confident in their talent and the ability to rock. And this was most evident in the fact that those original 30-minute sets had rapidly morphed into an hour or more, which allowed the band to expand far beyond the confines of the *Black Smoke Rising* material. "We had a lot of material that we were playing live," Jake reported to *AXS* some months into the tour. "There is a lot of material that we are playing live, a literal archive of material that we can pull from. The shows have all been original and different."

And as the tour progressed into July and August, Greta Van Fleet seemed to develop an almost Zen-like approach to the live performing experience. Yes it was, at the end of the day just rock 'n' roll. But in the minds of Greta Van Fleet it was becoming something existential, in a way that youngsters experiencing a lot new in their lives would couch it.

"I think the most important part in the band's evolution was that it does evolve," Dan offered *The Illinois Entertainer*. "We channel our youthful energy into everything we do. We're very tired after every show. We just like to work hard."

During that first tour, Greta Van Fleet would begin to experience the perks of budding stardom. There were those moments of fan hysteria that, occasionally, had band management devising elaborate plans to whisk their charges away from the insanity. There was also the matter of groupies which, at that point, was a murky subject. Young female fans were starting to come around and, according to reports of various veracity, all members of the band were unattached and quite happy with the attention of young women. But it was also plain that, on this first major tour, there really was no time for any serious mingling.

By September, the first leg of the 2017 tour was coming to an end. There would be some off days to recoup and reenergize before the band jumped back on the road for a mad dash to the end of the year. On September 7, the first phase of the band's personal and professional odyssey would literally come full circle when they were asked to be the opening act for legendary Detroit rocker Bob Seger in Saginaw, Michigan.

The occasion of that concert would literally be two ships passing in the night. Seger had previously announced that the current tour would be his last (although such "last tour" plans are notorious as being subject to change) while for Greta Van Fleet, this was the beginning, their first arena concert in front of a reported 16,000 fans. The significance of the show would not be lost on the band.

Pure and simple, GVF were massive fans of the veteran Detroit rock icon and came of age listening to Seger in his prime on local radio stations. If Greta Van Fleet had a bucket list, meeting and playing on the same bill with Bob Seger was number one and two on it. The band approached the show with equal parts excitement and, yes, nerves. They wanted to meet Seger, but they also wanted to be cool.

The day of the show, the band members showed up for their soundcheck and came face to face with their idol.

"He had just finished his soundcheck," Jake related to *Setlist.com*. "There he was, sitting down and playing 'Let It Be,' by himself, playing guitar and smoking a cigarette. We were like 'There's nothing that can beat it.' Finally, he finished and walked off and we walked up to him."

Dan recalled to *Setlist* that Seger's solo had eaten into their soundcheck. "He was like 'sorry boys' and we were like 'Nope! You're okay!'" Years later, Sam and Josh would collectively fill in the rest of the meeting in conversation with *Substream Magazine*. "To be there and see him, let alone meet him, was really special. He could have just said hello as he passed by but that's not what happened. He shook everyone's hand, looked each of us in the eye and introduced himself. He even asked for our names."

The euphoria of that meeting had Greta Van Fleet, figuratively walking on air through the rest of the day and later backstage at the concert. Then they were signaled to the stage. That's when the nerves kicked in.

"I remember the beginning of the show," Jake told *Loudwire.com*. "The lights in the arena were off and we could barely see each other. We knew how big a deal this was. It was our first arena show. I looked back at Danny and I could see that his hands were shaking.

"Then the lights came on."

Chapter Fifteen

From the Fires

The success of *Black Smoke Rising* and the early stages of the tour were both unexpected and overwhelming. There was not a reviewer or interviewer who was not falling all over themselves to proclaim Greta Van Fleet the next big thing. The good vibrations were circling the band like a flurry of angels. The band was thrilled. So was Lava Records. And while nobody was saying so publicly, privately everybody was speculating on what the next step should be. The overriding feeling was that it should be another album… And soon.

Greta Van Fleet had, among themselves, already been weighing the possibility of a new release. They had been writing new material like madmen both on and off tour and the result was they had more than enough releasable songs for two full albums. But they had reasons to proceed with caution.

In their minds, Greta Van Fleet felt they had unfinished business.

"Initially, the approach to that first EP was to showcase our range and variety of music," Jake related to *Go Venue Magazine*. "That range came from a different time and place." In the same interview, Dan said, "When we put together *Black Smoke Rising*, we thought that we were not finished with that thought."

Sam would be more critical of *Black Smoke Rising* as the prelude to what would become *From the Fires,* as he explained in *The Pop Break.com*. "We felt like *Black Smoke Rising* wasn't complete. It's a great EP but, from an artist's standpoint, we felt it was a little insular, one track and only one angle of Greta Van Fleet."

Which was why, rather than coming out with another EP, the band chose to dig deeper into their growing philosophy of heavy rock and humanity, a previously agreed-upon concept of eight songs—the four songs from *Black Smoke Rising* and four additional songs—two originals and two covers that worked, as a cohesive theme, to declare rock as both a social and political tool as well as a source of entertainment and emotion.

While "Highway Tune," "Safari Song," "Flower Power" and "Black Smoke Rising" were familiar, when staggered in presentation on the new EP, they would reconfigure into a new concept and message. The new material would consist of by now long-time concert staples "Talk On The Street" and "Edge Of Darkness," with two covers, a take on Sam Cooke's classic "A Change Is Gonna Come" and Fairport Convention's instrumentally and lyrically powerful "Meet On The Ledge."

The EP would be entitled *From the Fires* which, according to Josh in conversation *Loudwire.com* had its roots in a time-honored childhood tradition in the Kiszka household. "Our extended families and friends spent part of every summer together at a place called Yankee Springs. We were out in the middle of the woods and every night we'd sit around a campfire and play music and tell stories. It always reminded me of ancient times when people would gather around fires with the tribal elders, telling fables of wisdom and courage and passing down human history."

The four new songs were recorded at Rustbelt Studios during the band's September break from touring. Particular attention was being paid to recording the two covers, not only because Greta Van Fleet was anxious to put their own creative take on two of their favorite songs that they grew up with, but perhaps subconsciously they wanted to counter the ever-present Led Zeppelin critiques by proving their soul and folk influences ran equally deep. Of particular importance was getting "A Change Is Gonna Come," complete with some intriguing background choir vocals, where they wanted it.

"A Change Is Gonna Come" was a song that had always been sort of up in the air," Jake explained to *Go Venue* Magazine. "We had always enjoyed listening to it and had been wanting to do a cover. As a reflection of our times, we felt it played a great political importance. We felt it was an important time to record and release a song of that gravity."

Lava Records announced the release of *From the Fires* on October 25 with a scheduled November 10 drop. "Safari Song," the band's second single, was released on October 15. The song proved that Greta Van Fleet had gathered quite the following and was immediately acknowledged as the second most-added song on rock radio. *From The Fires* was greeted with equal enthusiasm, selling more than 104,000 albums in the US in less than four months. Consequently, *From The Fires* was all over US sales charts, hitting the *Billboard* Top 200 Album charts at No. 36, peaking at No. 4 at *Billboard's* Top Rock

Album charts and hitting No. 1 on *Billboard's* Top Hard Rock Album listings.

There was also a progression of sorts in the way critics were now responding to the band. Although they would never completely shake the Zeppelin comparison, reviewers were starting to get what Greta Van Fleet were all about, moving beyond the obvious and into the realm of insightful. *Anti Hero.com* acknowledged the band's growth, noting, "When you listen to *From the Fires*, you can clearly tell this group of young musicians have done their research and have created a sound that fits them well." *Spill Magazine.org* was also on board. "*From The Fires* blends the eight songs together making for a more comprehensive and cohesive flow. It was as if the album was written to be in this order." *Blues Rock Review* also waved the flag high. "*From The Fires* is a great continuation of where the band left off. For all the 'rock is dead' people out there, Greta Van Fleet is certainly proving that theory wrong. Rock 'n' roll doesn't need saving but Greta Van Fleet is certainly bringing it to a new generation."

If there was any surprise in the album's success it was how well *From the Fires* travelled internationally. *From the Fires* made appearances on the charts of 14 different countries outside the US. And the irony of ironies was that the band would receive its very first gold record certification from Poland.

It was a lot for Greta Van Fleet to drink in. But by the time the enormity of what was happening on the heels of *From the Fires* was sinking in, the band had long since packed their bags and were once again dishing it out to the masses on tour.

Chapter Sixteen

Add Ons

They found their itinerary growing by leaps and bounds. And the first sign that they had graduated to the big time was their wheels. Prior to ending the first phase of the 2017 tour, Greta Van Fleet was traveling budget-style, in a van and a trailer. But gearing up for leg two, the band suddenly found themselves in relative luxury, with two buses and a semi- truck.

By leg two, word of mouth and extensive airplay of *From the Fires* had resulted in additional shows being added in Los Angeles and New York. Of the former stop, shows at The Troubadour and The Moroccan Lounge were immediate sellouts and the demand was so great that the band wound up adding two more Troubadour shows, which reportedly sold out in five minutes. Not yet accustomed to the concept of selling out gigs in minutes and adding more nights, Greta Van Fleet were struggling to make sense of it all.

"The Troubadour shows sold out in five minutes," an amazed Sam told *Pollstar.com*. "That's just the craziest thing to me. It's just unbelievable that we're getting this kind of response."

Initial plans for the end of September had the band

booked for their very first European trip, a 10-day journey with stops in Germany, Paris, Amsterdam and the United Kingdom. But a last-second scheduling conflict with US dates forced the band to whittle down that portion of the tour to a mere two days in the UK, a September 26 show at the Black Heart Club and September 27 date at the Boston Music Room.

Landing in Heathrow Airport, Greta Van Fleet's 2017 triumph immediately took on an added sense of moment. Their first-ever trip outside the United States and the sights and sounds of London were washing over them in torrents. After all, this was the epicenter of much of the music and musicians who had formed the core of their musical upbringing, the place where many of their idols came to stardom and American blues legends found varying degrees of stardom after being largely ignored in the States. In a very big sense, London was home.

"I think it's really humbling, super exciting," Jake told *National Rock Review* prior to the London shows. "There's certainly an energy about being in London. I can't wait to get over there and start playing the shows. It's really exciting to be closer to it."

The excitement was palpable as they made their way to their very first gig in Europe, a small pub with an even smaller over-the-bar concert venue called Black Heart. Black Heart was an intimate space, not quite dive or hip, but an influential place with a liberal policy toward live performers. If you had talent, and were inclined toward the intimacy that a 150-seat capacity room offered, then the Black Heart was a good coming-out gig. For Greta Van Fleet, whose word of mouth and album sales in the UK were more than respectable, it was simply the next step.

Dan remembered the moment with *Classic Rock*.

"We were still at a point where we were still loading our own equipment. I think I must have carried every bit of my own equipment up the stairs in the Black Heart. We had so much adrenaline going that night."

The shows at Black Heart and Boston Music Room were a microcosm of Greta Van Fleet's reason for their mounting success. The performances were a mixture of talent and an adherence to hard rock tradition." It was literally a joyous noise, heavy rock played with passion, enthusiasm and an overriding sense of fun. The relatively small audiences got it and the band fed off it.

Greta Van Fleet returned to the States, caught a day of rest and, by October 1, were once again rocking in the USA. First stop" A fair-to-middling slot on what had become a so-so metal fest in which the band rubbed shoulders with Ozzy Osbourne, Rob Zombie, Mastodon, Incubus and more than two dozen others. The group were encouraged by the response they received despite being well down the bill, ultimately thrilled to be sharing a monster festival with many of their heavy rock idols.

The rest of October flew by with a non-stop array of support and headlining club shows, a handful of headlining small halls and another star-studded festival that saw the band logging stage time with Nine Inch Nails, Ozzy Osbourne and A Perfect Circle, among others. The remainder of the 2017 tour, which was by this time highlighted by sold-out shows at every stop, was conspicuous by its far-flung locations and long, often monotonous bus rides. But by their own estimation, Greta Van Fleet were handling the logistics of the tour just fine.

"I think we're very well built for this job," Sam told *LocalSpins.com*. "We're not really picky about where we sleep and we love travelling."

But Sam's comment was not completely accurate.

A long tour, combined with even a modicum of the rock 'n' roll lifestyle can cause issues. The members of Greta Van Fleet were nothing if not diligent in keeping their health up. It was known that they carried a daily vial of multivitamins with them at all times. The tour logistics did not offer much time for partying. But eating habits could often be sketchy at best. During the 2017 tour, at least two shows had to be cancelled because of illness.

By the time November rolled around, Greta Van Fleet were not well. Although the nature of their illness was never made specific, there had been reports of occasional bouts of laryngitis and sinus infections. Sam gave the band's prognosis in conversation with *Seattle Music Insider*. "We were about 14 dates (into the second leg of the 2017 tour) and then we all got sick. We had to cancel a lot of shows. There's nothing worse than being sick while on the road."

Unless we're talking mechanical difficulties.

The band was heading west in late October. Next stop: Sacramento, California. and the Aftershock Festival, which was rapidly becoming the hip place to play. The tour bus was barreling through the early morning hours. They were right on schedule when suddenly, at 2:30 a.m., the bus died. "Our tour bus broke down," Sam recalled in a *Setlist* interview. "Our tour manager had to stay up all night. We got in the car, packed our stuff in and drove five hours to Sacramento. Because we were late to the festival, the promoters had to move our slot to a later time. We had 15 minutes to move our shit to a different stage then the one we were supposed to be playing on and we ended up being the headliner."

There were no shows between November 3 and December 1. But the band was nothing if not busy.

There was the official unveiling of *From the Fires* and an increasing amount of press interest. The band managed to make it down to Tennessee for a bit of writing and recording. From the moment *From the Fires* was released, talk had gotten serious about the possibility of the first full-length album from Greta Van Fleet in the coming year, a speculation seemed fueled by the band's November studio time. Sam stopped short of announcing a new album but did acknowledge in a *Rat Rock News* conversation that the current studio time was scratching an itch. "Everyone's been requesting more material which is great to have that kind of response with people. I guess they're into it enough where we're kind of holding back from the touring and getting more into the studio. It's a difficult thing to juggle, going out to play shows and giving the people more material. It's a tough split but we're finding a happy medium right now."

There was the hanging out at home and getting into the Thanksgiving spirit and, in line with that, some rest and relaxation. But by December 1, the band was back on the road and into the home stretch of their coming out tour.

By now the last days of the 2017 tour had turned into a wonderful routine. Packed houses, electrifying performances, rave reviews and the overriding impression that Greta Van Fleet were leading a rock 'n' roll revolution, a happy return to those days of yesteryear.

By the time the band returned for a three-concert, year-end stand at Fox Theater in Detroit, they were beginning to experiment with their set list, supplementing the expected cuts from *Black Smoke Rising* and *From the Fires* with quite a few as-yet unreleased songs. Among those tunes new to even the most rabid fans were the acoustic "You're The One," a Fats Domino homage with a rendition of "Blueberry Hill"; the familiar strains of "Lover, Leaver, Taker Believer" in a rocking mash up with the Muddy Waters' classic "Rollin And Tumblin'"; and a riveting cover of Howlin Wolf's "Evil Is Goin' On."

Bringing in Christmas and the New Year on the highest of highs, Greta Van Fleet were a youthful mixture of exhilarated, humbled and amazed at the good fortune Santa had brought them in 2017. "This year has been overwhelming," Jake told *How Was It Detroit?.com* "The venues have been getting bigger and the crowds have been growing. What can you say except overwhelming?"

Chapter Seventeen

They've Got a Fan in Me

Jake remembers it like it was yesterday.

"I remember the moment," Jake told *Rock 95* and countless other media outlets. "It was about 10 a.m. and management calls and says, 'You have a call coming from England in a little while.' So we pick up the phone and the voice on the other end says 'Hey boys! It's Elton.' It was actually Elton John on the phone."

Elton John, in the midst of what was being called his retirement tour, had heard Greta Van Fleet's music and become an immediate fan. "They were the best rock and roll I've heard in 20 fucking years," he enthused to various outlets, including *Loudwrire.com*.

For Jake, talking to Elton that morning was a literal blast from the past. The Kiszka brothers, thanks to their mother, had grown up mesmerized by the music of Elton John. To say that the singer/songwriter was a major influence was a massive understatement. The reason Elton had called would momentarily put the icing on the cake for Greta Van Fleet: He asked if they would be interested in performing at that year's annual Elton John's Academy Awards charity after-party. Once they agreed, the band members immediately called their mothers with variations of "you're not going to believe this."

It was a fairy tale that would have a kicker. During that initial conversation, Elton offered an added bonus. Elton said, "You know, I still play music and, if you'd like, I'd love to play a song with you guys or maybe two,'" Dan recalled in *The Illinois Entertainer*. "He would end up learning 'You're The One' during the soundcheck the night of the show."

The band spent the next few weeks working up what would ultimately be an hour set. They were nervous. Playing for Elton John and a room full of upper-class celebrities and socialites was not the typical Greta Van Fleet audience. The night of the party their set list consisted of "Edge Of Darkness," "You're The One," and the Elton John chestnut "Saturday Night's Alright For Fighting," the latter two songs with the capable assistance of Sir Elton John himself.

As the band took the stage, amidst the glitz and glamour of Hollywood, Elton John was effusive in introducing them. "They blew me away. You're gonna see them here. They're gonna be one of the biggest new bands of the year."

Greta Van Fleet had never been so nervous and excited in their lives. The set was a masterful success with the band and Elton John showing major rock chops to an enthusiastic audience of the Hollywood's elite. After the performance, in a private moment with the band, Elton became a teacher of sorts, offering a bit of sage advice to the band.

"Elton told us, 'you guys are young,'" Jake told *GQ Magazine*. "He said 'you've got to flaunt it.' That's when I went from wearing T-shirts to wearing half-cut jackets with nothing underneath. If Elton John tells you to flaunt it, no one else can tell us otherwise."

How much better could 2018 be? Greta Van Fleet were about to find out.

The mania for the band had taken on gigantic proportions. A first leg of the 2018 tour, which was scheduled to run from March to June, had been an immediate sellout. Potentially more important was the fact that 14 of those dates took in a European tour of The Netherlands, Amsterdam, Germany, Belgium, Paris, England and Scotland, which also sold out well in advance of the tour kickoff, a sure sign that the band was growing on a large-scale, international level.

The audience response to the band indicated that rock had no borders. Fans knew the lyrics and songs. The concept of a band based largely in influences well before they were born was new and exciting. It was an excitement was easily matched by the band experiencing the rest of the world for the first time. "It was amazing," Sam told *Ultimate Classic Rock* in a philosophical moment. "We were going places that we had never been before, literally and figuratively, touring the world and having all these experiences."

But the bassist would flip on a dime when he told *Pittsburgh Music Magazine* that their reaction overseas and elsewhere boiled down to something more primal. "We love making music and we love playing shows. But we never expected anything like the attention we've been getting."

Greta Van Fleet finished up the European leg of the tour on April 5 and immediately launched into the meat and potatoes portion of the US leg of the tour, two sold-out performances at the famed John Anson Ford Amphitheater in Los Angeles (April 16 and 17), sandwiched in between three appearances over two weeks at the Coachella Music Festival (April 13, 14 and 20).

The Coachella shows had become notorious for mixing and matching all manner of commercial and alternative performers, and Greta Van Fleet was both excited and anxious at the prospect of playing among their peers and idols. They were particularly anxious to share the stage with two of their folk-oriented favorites, First Aid Kit and Fleet Foxes. Unfortunately, on the April 13 show, a mid-afternoon set inside a tent, they found that many of the performing basics they'd become used to were not available to them.

In a conversation with *Setlist FM,* Sam and Jake explained the hoops they jumped through. "It was rather difficult with our stage Weekend 1. "We had no sound check. We had no line check. It was run and gun. They threw our equipment on stage for that first time and said, 'Get up and play.' And that's all we had. Because of the technical difficulty and the lack of any sound check or anything, it was like just walking out and being in that one moment."

Their second appearance at Coachella the following day went much better and, most importantly, Josh's vocals seemed to be showing no signs of slacking amidst the grind of belting out over-the-top blues vocals on a near-nightly basis, which, truth be known, had become a quietly talked about issue on the current tour. The band, collectively, had been adhering to a healthy road regimen, eating as healthily as possible and taking all manner of multi vitamins in an attempt to keep the Greta Van Fleet train rolling.

But as they bided their time in Los Angeles before their next Coachella appearance with the first of two sold-out shows at the John Anson Ford Amphitheater, Josh, according to reports, was not feeling right. Nevertheless, the band did the April 16 show and, while it appeared that Josh was dragging at times, he was belting out the band's anthems with the expected, high-octane range. But whatever was bothering him (allegedly vocal issues) would worsen overnight and the band was forced to cancel the second John Anson Ford date. But Josh made a miraculous recovery over the next three days, and Greta Van Fleet were able to perform the final weekend of Coachella on April 20.

The band continued to crisscross the US through the month of May. It was obvious that progress was being made. Small concert halls and larger arenas had come with their rapid ascendancy up the rock star ladder. The band was typically playing in front of 3-5,000 fans on any given night. The groundwork had been laid by the beginning of June for an even larger second leg of the 2018 tour that would take them through the rest of the year.

Now it was time for Greta Van Fleet to drop a much-anticipated bomb.

Chapter Eighteen

One Week in a Haunted Cabin

It was 2018 and Greta Van Fleet were finally ready. The EP's and a mammoth amount of touring had paved the way. It was time for a magnum opus, their *Sgt. Pepper's Lonely Hearts Club Band*, if one might be so bold. *Anthem of the Peaceful Army* would be really something, they boasted to reporters. But privately there would be some doubt as to just exactly what it would be.

Initially the band's plan had been to empty out a large amount of previously written songs, according to Sam in a *Loudwire* interview. "We had all these songs that we had written three to five years ago that we were just going to put on the album."

But when the band went down to Nashville in January, to do some writing and recording with the now familiar production team of Sutton, Young and Boone, they suddenly saw the light. "When we got to the studio, we thought we were going to use all the songs we recorded or wrote over the past five years," Sam recalled in *Music Connection*. "But then we started playing them and they were too simple. We were kind of disappointed."

Maturity and experience had a lot to do with losing interest in older songs. So did a confluence of social and philosophical views along with personal insights and growth. It began to bubble over one night when Greta Van Fleet's tour bus was rocketing down the highway, and Josh was jolted from a fitful sleep.

"The idea came to me one morning," Josh told *Uproxx.com*. "I guess I was in a state of meditation. I had these thoughts and words coming to me. I jumped out of bed and I had to write something down."

The resultant poem that emerged from Josh's subconscious, *Anthem of the Peaceful Army*, laid out a broad scenario of humanity being interconnected, all part of a global community. But Sam would recall, that as the loosely defined concept album began to take shape, the ideas came into sharper focus and would run deep.

"It's a concept album that kind of dives into roots and beliefs," Sam explained to *Blabbermouth.net*. "I think it asks very large questions. What are we doing to ourselves? What are we doing to our environment? What are we doing to each other? Why must there be hate? Why must there be evil and greed?"

For his part, Jake, in the same interview, saw the concept of the album, in esoteric terms, as an opportunity to advance musically. "A lot came from inventing instrumental voicings and shapes. At a certain point, I started going somewhere else other than the blues licks I've always played. In doing that, a lot of obscure things happened as far as the guitar goes, like licks that don't really have an identity. A lot of that was happening. A lot of experimentation and a lot of creative freedom."

With sudden, wide-ranging interests brewing in the band's collective psyche, what had originally been seen as a fairly easy recording session where older songs would make up the bulk of the album, Greta Van Fleet were now talking a wider-ranging language, one that would take longer than originally expected. But it would be a delay that everybody agreed would be worth the wait.

With the start of the first leg of the 2018 tour looming on the horizon, the band, throughout January and into February, went to Nashville…

… And almost immediately disappeared.

Their destination? An isolated cabin in the mountains of Chattanooga, Tennessee, an hour from the nearest town. The cabin had an unobstructed view of the nearby mountain ranges and was within walking distance of a nearby graveyard. Sam, in conversation with *Premier Guitar.com,* recalled the journey to the middle of nowhere.

"You drive out of Nashville for about two hours and you see nothing, nothing, nothing. And then there was this winding road that went up for about 20 minutes. We got to this cabin and it looked kind of small and raggedy. But we go in and it's just pure beauty with spiral staircases. You walk out on this massive balcony and you see trillions of trees. It was amazing."

And it was in the midst of extreme isolation that Greta Van Fleet found the ideal place to create new music for *Anthem of the Peaceful Army*. "We wanted to get out into more of a wilderness setting," Josh recalled in *Rolling Stone*. "Because that's where we knew that things would become clear."

Once settled in, the band began a regimented routine designed to put their new ideas and thoughts into reality. They would begin work promptly at noon, writing and recording primitive demos until well past midnight. Creative sessions would often turn spiritual, as Josh recalled in *Rolling Stone*. "Jake would get nice and drunk, go out on the balcony and talk to the spirits. He was talking into space like nothing existed."

Adding to the surreal nature of that week in the cabin was the growing perception that their hideaway was definitely haunted. Jake would acknowledge to *Premier Guitar* that there was definitely a ghostly vibe about the place. "We went into the basement once and that was the last time any of us stepped into the basement." Josh was more direct in his assessment when he told *Rolling Stone,* "If there was a haunted fucking cabin, that would be the one."

And they would discover the spirits were particularly active when the band members were working. Jake recalled one night in particular, after the rest of the band had gone to bed, that he stayed up alone to work on some mixes in the living room area. But as he would tell *Premier Guitar.com*, he was not alone.

"Everyone else was in bed but I could hear, very clearly, footsteps walking behind me. My whole body went cold and I just got goosebumps. I thought the other guys had come downstairs, but I turned around and nothing was there. The footsteps would continue throughout the rest of the night and finally I said 'Stop. Leave me alone. I'm trying to work.' All of a sudden it (the footsteps) stopped."

Jake was not the only one to encounter spirits. Dan was asleep one day while the rest of the band was outside. He would later report that every time one of the brothers would tell a joke, he would hear a little girl's voice laughing.

Being at the cabin had an influence on the writing going on at that point. Jake acknowledged as much when he talked about the origin of the song "Age Of Man." "It was the perfect area to be in. Being in isolation definitely set the mood for that song. It started as a riff and an arrangement and eventually grew into something epic."

It had been a given that Greta Van Fleet would return to familiar grounds at Detroit's Rustbelt Studios to record their first full length album. But a lot had changed for the band in the course of a year, and those changes, professional and personal, would necessitate a relocation to Blackbird Studios in Nashville. Nashville was where their management was located and would be central to doing press and prepping for the second part of what was shaping up as a mammoth second leg of the 2018 tour. Personal reasons also played in to the move to Blackbird, according to a conversation with producer Marlon Young in *Sound On Sound.com*.

"We all have the same issues when we're in Detroit," he said. "My son needing me or somebody's wife or girlfriend needing attention. In Detroit there were a lot of distractions. We were in Nashville for one purpose only and that was to make a good record."

In line with that, a regimented and streamlined recording schedule was set up around touring requirements. Initial recording sessions were set in increments of ten and seven days followed by another four days to finish vocals.

By the time Greta Van Fleet had returned from their week in the haunted cabin, the band was literally up to their eyeballs in music, with reportedly as many as 41 songs in various stages of development. Anxious to begin a whittling-down process, Sutton, Young and Boone set up a couple of microphones and recorded the band playing every song they had. From there, it was a matter of reducing the number of songs down to a manageable level for what was presumed to be no more than 12 songs for the proposed album.

The process of selecting which songs would make the cut would be chaotic. The producers would offer their two cents but ultimately, the final selection would boil down to the band, and that democracy did have its moments. "The process of selecting the songs was chaos," Sam told *Music Connection*. "It was everybody speak their mind at once and speak freely without holding back."

During the recording process for *Anthem of the Peaceful Army*, the band continued to be near-manic in the exploration of this batch of songs and, along the way, creating new, viable music to add to the mix. A new song, "Brave New World," was created in the studio, while the band would redo what would become a now-familiar riff on the song "When The Curtain Falls."

Familiarity between the band and producers made for a smooth shorthand as the album progressed. "Our arrangement suggestions were minimal," recalled producer Young to *Sound On Sound.com*. "We talked about things like tempos, arrangements and song structures. But by the time the band came into the studio, the songs were fully written and the arrangements were all pretty close."

The band's creative inclinations continued to be all over the place. Some elements of the recordings were well thought out in advance, while others would prove to be spur-of-the-moment inspiration. In-studio experimentation resulted in a lap steel guitar playing an important role in the creation of the song "Anthem." Rummaging around in the instrument collection at Blackbird inspired Jake to play a guitar modified to make sitar-type sounds that would be employed on the song 'Watching Over.'

By the end of February, *Anthem of the Peaceful Army*

was for all intents and purposes complete. Which was just as well, because the second phase of their 2018 tour was set to start in March. But there were those nagging last-minute bits, primarily vocal and instrumental overdubs, that needed to be plugged in. Consequently, March was a bit of a wild ride as, between shows in both North America and Europe, the band would race back to Detroit and Rustbelt Studios, a day here and a day there, to tweak the tracks for an album that Greta Van Fleet would readily admit was "for them."

But while the rollercoaster ride to complete *Anthem of the Peaceful Army* was in full flower, Josh told the *Detroit Free Press* that the process was all good. "Ultimately, all the distractions helped. The album captured the chaos."

But like any overtly ambitious project from a fairly young band, Greta Van Fleet did have some doubts and tension surrounding the recording of *Anthem of the Peaceful Army*.

There was the seemingly endless quest for quality material, with much of that search couched in doubt and perfection, and whether or not their first full album would top their previous efforts. Jake was well aware of those concerns in conversation with *Undercover Music.com*. "A few times we looked at each other and thought 'this is moving at a pace and really going somewhere beyond our expectations.'"

There was also the question of whether, creatively, Greta Van Fleet might be overstepping things. That concern was on the mind of Josh when he talked to the *Detroit Free Press*. "What we're doing is sincere and, hopefully, not any bit pretentious. If you don't do it right, you're really screwed. You can come off as just pretentious if you're aiming high and just don't make it."

Recording *Anthem of the Peaceful Army* would generate quite a bit in the way of creative tensions. It would often be a discussion that turned into an argument, based on youthful enthusiasm versus the reality of the recording studio process. One of those decisions that would cause Danny some sleepless nights was the recording of the song "Lover Leaver Taker Believer." In the studio it was laid out as a six-minute song. But it had already proven a crowd-pleasing jam piece in a live setting that would often last 20 minutes. Dan explained the conundrum to *Drum!.com*.

"We could have recorded the track in sections but we really wanted to jam it out in one take. Live, the song changes so much from night to night and I was thinking 'Okay, how am I going to pack all these sections in and make it sound aggressive but natural?'" The band would ultimately be satisfied with the studio version. "Hey, that's great. But I really could have done it better with one more try. But you know, we were just getting started making records."

And even if the band voiced concerns, Greta Van Fleet was ultimately satisfied with the finished product. Even to the point of arrogance, as exhibited by Sam and Josh in an animated give and take with *Metrotimes.com*. "We've never really paid much attention to how our music is received. It's just how we think. Is it done? Is it good? Is this as close as we can get? I think that's what we're mostly worried about. If the album tanks, we could probably give a shit. You know what I mean? It's just music. If it all ends tomorrow, we'll just move on."

Chapter Nineteen

Playing in a Traveling Band

As Greta Van Fleet prepared to return to the road, they were mentally checking boxes. Clothes? Check. Instruments? Check. Passports? Check. But the reality of setting off on yet another long tour over many months brought up some realities. And a big one was that, as their star rose in the rock skies, they were rarely home for longer than a couple of days. But while they missed being in Frankenmuth and being around family and old friends, the band saw it as part and parcel of the rock 'n' roll life.

"You think about never being home," Sam reflected in a *Bass Player* interview. "Living in tour buses, Airbnb's, hotels, studios. There's no time to be home, ever. There's so much to do. There are not enough hours in the day. It's a lot of pressure but it's also a hell of a lot of fun."

And feeding into the fun were the reports that nearly all the upcoming shows through the end of the year were sold out, the capacity for the shows had almost doubled, *and* new dates and larger venues were constantly being added. These reports were feeding their mania for playing for the people. Sam summed those feelings up succinctly when he told *Consequence of Sound.com,* "Getting in front of people with our music is what it's all about. We've always been a live band. That's what we do."

And to a large extent music was becoming all they did. They had arrived at a point all bands strive for: making their passion their life. Greta Van Fleet were now officially caught up in the cycle of celebrity and stardom. And they were running toward it rather than away from it. They were making their lives and their passion work on a grand stage.

The tour was shaping up as a marathon, kicking off in Europe with stops in The Netherlands, Amsterdam, Germany, Belgium, Paris, Scotland, England before a return to the States, their first shows in Canada, and then a return to Europe. This would be Greta Van Fleet's life through the end of 2018.

Not surprisingly, and most likely as a buffer to road weariness, the band had boiled down the road to a mental and philosophical equation. Preparing to play each night before thousands of people was now as simple as getting into a positive state of mind. Once this nightly ritual was complete and Greta Van Fleet hit the stage, the rest was just plain fun.

Sam told *Music Connection* that the evolution of the band's touring attitude inevitably revolved around their forms of transportation. "We didn't realize that touring could be so easy. When things started getting more serious, we upgraded to a van. That van was a rolling deathtrap and it only lasted about four months. Then we upgraded to a bus. It's more complex but easier. The only thing that's consistent on the road these days is the time we're scheduled to show up for a soundcheck prior to a show."

The first full-blown tour of Europe, starting in March

and continuing into early April, was significant on a number of levels. Greta Van Fleet's going across the pond was the mirror image of The British Invasion of America in the '60s. The mania for the band in Europe was palpable, fans of all ages were embracing the band as both the next big thing and an exciting return to a kind of heavy music that had seemingly gone the way of the dinosaurs, but was once again emerging as vibrant and relevant.

The result was that Europe hailed Greta Van Fleet as conquering heroes. A much-improved lighting and stage presence served rather than detracted from the primal nature of their performance. Their four-piece lineup showed the power as reinvented by a bunch of young kids who were not even born when heavy rock first roamed the earth. Shows were universally praised. The band was in their element, playing live.

For Greta, the European portion of the tour was jam-packed, and allowed little time for them to play the tourist game. But going overseas had done wonders in opening up the possibilities of a future that could only be envisioned by youth. In a tweet following the conclusion of the European leg, the band wrote, "Thank you for an unforgettable run in Europe. We will never forget the breathtaking sights and sounds."

Then it was a quick hop back to the States, where a long trip on a superhighway of headlining shows and festival dates awaited them. Dan would wax near-poetic as he described their return to the US in a *Coachella Weekly* conversation. "We flew in from across the world, trying to adjust to an 11-hour time difference. We were just in a whole different place, a completely different culture and then we were on a plane and on a stage. It was like time travelling."

After the show at the John Anson Ford Amphitheater and Coachella, Greta Van Fleet's performance had begun to solidify. The set was now clocking in at about 90 minutes. The lights were strategically placed around the stage, not too over the top, and designed to enforce the live nature of the songs and the performance.

Typical of the maturing stage presence was the May 23 show at the Fillmore in Detroit. The show was a homecoming of sorts; all 2,800 seats were sold out in record time. The set saw Greta Van Fleet at their rocking best, emphasizing the emotion in each song with physical and vocal gyrations. To a large extent, the set was pretty much rote, songs from *Black Smoke Rising* and *From the Fires* mixed with a couple of teasers from their upcoming album. But the band was not above tweaking expectations. "Highway Tune," which had long been regulated to the show closer, turned up as the very first song this night and would occasionally open the show throughout the remainder of the tour. Of particular note was the way that the band had reconfigured the structure of "Lover Leaver Taker Believer" into a showstopper of a jam session that would run as much as 20 minutes and allow Greta Van Fleet to showcase their true rock chops in a primal, forceful manner.

May and June brought a run of festival appearances such as Hangout Festival and Carolina Rebellion. For Greta Van Fleet these were the fun times which often brought out the small boy in them. They were hanging around countless big-name performers and were appropriately in awe of the company they were now keeping. In describing their festival experience, Sam offered that there was definitely a difference between sharing a stage with dozens of other bands and headlining their own shows.

"There's a lot of pressure when we go up for our own

shows," Sam told *AXS.com.* "When we're at a festival everybody is giving a part to help make something great. Doing a festival, it's like the whole thing isn't on our back. The sets are shorter so we can cut loose and have a lot of fun."

The June 24 makeup show at the John Anson Ford Amphitheater was of some significance in terms of in which way the band was moving. Among all the expected hits and familiar songs, a large portion of the set was given over to new songs off the upcoming *Anthem of the Peaceful Army,* which still had no release date. It was a subtle bit of business to gauge interest in the new material but, most importantly, it was giving the band a change of pace from what had become a by-the-numbers set list. In typical Greta Van Fleet fashion, the band could do no wrong.

Into July, the long-promised Canadian shows would come to pass. Over the course of a week, Greta Van Fleet would headline several area shows, including a blowout at Toronto's Famed Velvet Underground Club and two nights at that city's popular REBEL nightclub. But the crown jewel of their Canadian trip would be July 9, the much-anticipated multi-day Festival d'ete Quebec in Quebec City, which traditionally drew an estimated 100,000 music lovers a day. And as it would turn out the band would play right before the day's headliners The Foo Fighters. As usual, Greta Van Fleet were hopped up and deep into the concept of not only playing on the same stage as one of their idols but performing before a crowd that would ultimately be estimated at 90,000 fans. But as Jake would reflect in *Premier Guitar*, the gods would add their own element to the moment to their song "Lover Leaver, Taker Believer."

"In front of us were about 90,000 people. All you could see was the people from the front of the stage to the back. All of a sudden it started raining right in the middle of our set, it started raining and the crowd just went insane. You could hear them singing the lyrics as we were playing the song. Right in the middle of the song we started jamming. We could feel their energy. We were like 'alright! Let's do this! We were altogether in this!' I started ripping a solo. The crowd was yelling my name."

Chapter Twenty

When the Curtain Falls

Greta Van Fleet stuck around Canada just long enough to pick up gold record awards commemorating sales of the EP *From the Fires* and the song "Highway Tune" north of the border. It's always been a record industry tradition to honor past glories and, as they smiled broadly and drank celebratory champagne before the cameras during the awards presentation, Greta Van Fleet would project their humble feelings about the honor. Whether they agreed with the concept or not, the band recognized that gold records were a sign of accomplishment and industry acceptance, so they took in the moment. But already their minds were set on the next gig and, in many instances, the ongoing question of when their first full-length album would land.

Depending on their mood at the moment or the tone of the interview, the band's responses to the album release question would range from charges that the press "was poking and prodding," as was the case in a *KROQ* radio interview, to Sam's tongue-in-cheek reply that "it was none of your business," to Josh's more tempered response to *MLive.com:* "We're reshaping it and getting it into mastering. Hopefully we'll release it soon."

But the reality was that "soon" was nowhere in sight

and another prediction that it would be released in late summer was looking more and more unlikely. Truth be known, if it was up to the band, *Anthem of A Peaceful Army* would have already been released. But the reality was that, behind the scenes, there was a record label and management team that was doing the mental math and configuring the best time to release the album for maximum impact. And by the beginning of summer they must have realized that it was time to toss Greta Van Fleet fans a bone.

And so on July 17, "When The Curtain Falls" was released. It began with a riff and a rudimentary arrangement. "Then it was a pretty quick process," Jake told *Billboard*. "As soon as I played the riff and the arrangement, everybody knew what they had to do and we worked the whole thing out in about 15 minutes."

Adding to the potency of the song was a clever, minimalist video in which the band members made their way up a mountainous, alien-looking desert landscape, plugged their instruments into jacks miraculously projecting out of rock outcroppings and banged out the song. A series of quick camera cuts through a Super 8 filter created the desired vintage '70 s look. Very simple and subtly psychedelic, "When The Curtain Falls" was an instant video hit on Spotify.

On the surface it all seemed like the ideal tease for the much-anticipated album. The song definitely played to Greta Van Fleet's perceived strengths. Thick and heavy instrumentals relied on heavy distorted guitar riffs by Jake, a thundering bottom was provided by Sam and Dan and, perhaps most identifiable, the shrieking impassioned vocals and mystical lyrics that explored the irony of the human soul and psyche. For better or worse, there was no getting away from the fact that the song sounded a lot like a certain band whose comparison to Greta Van Fleet seemed never-ending.

The band was irritated at the prospect of "When The Curtain Falls" opening up yet another round of comparisons to Zeppelin. So when the inevitable questions would come, Greta Van Fleet made strong attempts to intellectualize rather than get upset. Sam seemed particularly adept at deflecting Led Zeppelin questions in a more mindful way, as he offered in interviews with *Vulture.com* and *Billboard*.

"It's an innate human instinct to compare, contrast and to make things more relatable. I really feel like the whole Led Zeppelin thing has died down in the past six months. Which is nice, because I'm getting tired of answering these questions. The new music has its sound and it's very Greta Van Fleet. People tend to think of Greta Van Fleet as loud, fast, hard rock 'n' roll music. But there's a lot more to it than that. In making this new album, we spread out and touched the corners of what Greta Van Fleet is."

And what Greta Van Fleet continued to be was a band whose music constantly had people choosing sides.

It came as no surprise that "When The Curtain Falls" was all over the place critically. Even those who liked the song often fell back on Zeppelin references. But while mixed, reviewers were generally positive and willing to give the song the benefit of the doubt. *Billboard* described the sound as "as hard hitting drums, funky guitar solos and sky high impassioned vocals." *Rolling Stone* called the song "swaggering and blistering with a bluesy guitar and bass melody." *Variety* noted that the song, "like much of the band's music, has a sound similar to Led Zeppelin." *Metal Sucks.com* offered a youthful, gonzo assessment when it offered, "It's pretty good if you like Led Zeppelin. It's hard to imagine you won't like this, so crank it and enjoy."

"When The Curtain Falls" would go on to have an interesting chart life. Charting on *Billboard's* US Hot Rock Songs and US Rock Airplay listings was to be expected. But having a life on both the Belgian and Bolivian charts would only be a pleasant surprise, albeit one that would most certainly attest to the international world's appetite for heavy rock.

The song would also find life in the video and multi-media universe, appearing on the soundtrack for the *NHL 19* video game and in Vol. 9 of Coheed and Cambria's ongoing musical story telling odyssey *The Amory Wars: Unheavenly Creatures*.

But the real moment for Greta Van Fleet and "When The Curtain Falls" would arrive ten days after the release of the song when, on July 26, the band would essentially premiere it on television for the first time on *The Tonight Show Starring Jimmy Fallon*, the latest incarnation of that decades-long late night television staple. It would be one song, but Greta Van Fleet took it upon themselves to make "When The Curtain Falls" an experience. They brought their own lighting to the show to enhance that '70 s vibe and they dressed to the nines in their trademark hippie/mystical outfits.

But at the end of the day, it boiled down to the band and their mad skills. Even in the relative confines of a television studio, the foursome brought a loud, live concert experience with raging guitar work and roaring vocals. By the time the band finished "When The Curtain Falls," people in the audience who had not been born in the '70s knew what it must have felt like.

Show host Jimmy Fallon succinctly summed up the experience when he enthusiastically tweeted "You guys crushed it!"

Chapter Twenty-One

It Is What It Is

By the end of July, there was a sense that Greta Van Fleet had finally arrived.

Not in terms of record sales and sold-out concerts, although those material aspects were nothing to sneeze at.

But one only had to look at the still very young musicians to realize that they were now very much adults. You could see it in the way they conducted themselves in the media and business world, the way they walked the walk and talked the talk. While it did not show on their faces, there was a growing sense of experience about them. They had done a lot in only a few years, survived it all, and were poised to do it all over again. Greta Van Fleet were giving every indication in their acts and deeds that they were not in it for the short haul, and as they were preparing to take the *Anthem of the Peaceful Army* tour through the rest of 2018, they were nothing if not aware of what they were all about.

Prior to departing on the second leg of the tour, which would take in both international and north American shows, Dan got to the meat of the matter in a conversation with *New Jersey Arts.com*. "We're becoming more of a live band and a different kind of show," he offered. "We're upping our tour game. Now the audience can expect an experience to develop and a whole lot of noise."

He would go on to explain how experience had definitely been the best teacher. "Each of these shows is like an actual milestone that you get to experience. Everything is just happening so quickly. Once we played a show for a thousand people, it seemed easier to do it again. Meeting some of the people that we've met, all these different types of people, helps. Once you've done it, it's easier to do it again."

With the remaining shows through November already sold out, the Fall schedule for the *Anthem of the Peaceful Army* tour was shaping up as a victory lap with little, in a commercial sense, left to prove. But the band steadfastly insisted that the challenges they faced were a constant. And so while the Japan Sonic Festival and Chicago's Lollapalooza Festival would be eye-opening exercises in spectacle complete with a supporting cast of thousands, Greta Van Fleet maintained an almost purist attitude in which success was based on the power of their music and the ability to connect with the rock 'n' roll masses. For the band, being in the rock 'n' roll world had taken on an almost metaphysical and societal link.

It would take an ultra-deep and cerebral publication, *Psychology Today*, to attempt to make sense of it all, painting a convincing picture of Greta Van Fleet as a musical conduit attempting to unite multi-generational masses at a time when government and corporate greed and corruption were pointing a way to disillusionment and hopelessness. The publication tracked down Josh to get the reasoning behind the larger aspects of Greta Van Fleet. Josh was seemingly the ideal candidate to probe deeper meanings and during the conversation, often went into thoughtful philosophical discourse. But he was also able to make a straightforward case as to what Greta Van Fleet and their music portended for their fans and the future.

"The visceral stuff in our music seems to be rooted in an ancient society. There's something really primeval about shrieking, making noises and beating on drums (which in essence is what Greta Van Fleet is about). I'm kind of relieved that people are getting what our music is talking about. Certain themes are starting to register. People are starting to understand this world. People have been writing us saying 'I didn't feel like I belonged in this world or this generation. But the music has given me purpose.'"

In early September, Greta Van Fleet ended the anticipation when they announced that *Anthem of a Peaceful Army* would be released on October 19. To further generate interest, the band began a timed rollout of the cuts "Lover, Leaver Taker Believer"(September 21), "Anthem" (October 21) and "You're The One" (October 16).

In the days leading up to the release of the album, the band continued to be readily available to talk up their latest effort. Jake, in separate interviews with *Billboard* and *Blues Rock Review*, stoked the interest. "I think there's some maturity on this album that, musically, you can hear. We were able to take our time and try new arrangements and new writing techniques. It's very energetic and aggressive. I see this album as a big picture look at where we are now and where we're headed."

Anthem of the Peaceful Army was a smash right out of the box, selling an estimated 85,000 copies in its first week of release, and debuting at No. 3 on the *Billboard* rock charts. That was to be expected.

What the band, their record label, management and fans did not expect was that the album would turn Greta Van Fleet into one of the most polarizing bands of the decade, bringing long-simmering knocks against the band raging to the surface. Reviews were, to be generous, mixed. Some were dismissive and some were downright vicious in holding the album and the band up as a symbol of a corporate recording industry at its worst.

Classic Rock offered that *Anthem of the Peaceful Army* was "One of the most exciting records released by a new band in recent years, partly because of the amount of money and attention thrown at them. This is the first time in years that a rock band has been given a major fighting chance by a major label." *Esquire* took a more rambling discourse in its review, citing the uncoolness of the band even as they were attempting to be cool and acknowledging while the band did have talent, they were essentially not mature enough for the mantle of true greatness. The actual music was bad and the band's entire aesthetic disingenuous because it was released by a major label.

But it remained for a scathing review by the website *Pitchfork* to literally have Greta Van Fleet fans choosing sides. "Greta Van Fleet sound like they did weed exactly once, called the cops and tried to record a Led Zeppelin album before they arrested themselves. They care so deeply and are so precious with their half-baked boomer fetishism that they mollycoddled every impulse of '60s rock 'n' roll into an interminable 49-minute drag. They don't even realize that they are more of an algorithmic fever dream than an actual rock band."

The band's supporters would be equally vehement in their attacks on the review and in their support of the band.

One irate Van Fleet fan would go so far as to suggest that the bad review was payback for one of the band members having sex with the reviewer's girlfriend. But it would remain for cooler heads, in the guise of the band themselves, to address the *Pitchfork* put down.

Josh told *Rolling Stone* that "It's unfortunate they'd be putting that energy out into the world but that's their prerogative. I'd like to think there's some substance to what we're doing." Sam had similar sentiments when speaking to *Ultimate Guitar.com*. "I don't know the intent behind the piece. I'm not sure if it's a publication trying to get attention or if it's somebody who genuinely doesn't like us and what we're doing. I really don't think we get too worked up about it. If you can't do it, I guess then you just write about it. I feel like this man has had a troubled past. Prayers up for him."

Greta Van Fleet would ultimately turn out to be the Teflon rockers when it came to critics who would be vastly outnumbered by fans. Besides *Billboard*, where the band would ultimately rise to No. 1 on the rock charts, *Anthem of the Peaceful Army* would land on 17 international charts and quickly be certified Gold in Poland and Canada.

The year would continue to see growth for the band in the area of music licensing. Heavy rock had become the new hip element to add mood to movies and television, and Greta Van Fleet was right there to take advantage, placing "Highway Tune" in the soundtracks of the movie *Den of Thieves*, and an episode of the television series *Preacher* and "Safari Song" in the big-budget DC Comics movie *Aquaman*.

But when all the hoopla and controversy surrounding the creative merits of Greta Van Fleet began to fade, the band was already back on the road, continuing to test the touring waters both nationally and internationally. That the road was finally their proving ground as Josh discussed world tours with *Gulf Times*. "People just have to let us know if they want to see us live. If the demand is there, we'll come and play."

Chapter Twenty-Two

Say Goodbye to 2018

Sex, drugs and rock 'n' roll. It's an age-old acknowledgement of the rock lifestyle that has always been a true test of life on the road. However, on tour Greta Van Fleet's personal lives were fairly monastic.

According to reports, the closest thing to band members having sex on the road has been occasional bras and ladies undergarments thrown on the stage. Oh, the band members are quick to acknowledge the presence of groupies on tour, but then tend to go philosophical by not giving a definitive yes or no. Drugs? Bet the farm no, although there is much evidence to indicate that Greta Van Fleet are not above chugging a beer or two in their off hours. The rock 'n' roll is a given. The boys in the band rock and rock hard. And yes, these rock gods are truly mortal. In an interview with *Guitar Girl Magazine* prior to going out on the final leg of the 2018, Jake conceded that fatigue was a constant companion.

"We tend to have a day or three off in between shows. You get to a certain point where it's like you're totally out of energy and so you begin to look forward to those days off. I would say that our age in this circumstance is an advantage. All we really have to do is rock 'n' roll."

And that's what the band would be doing in spades. Their popularity was now worldwide. Shows were immediately selling out and additional shows were being added. In the truest sense of the word, the final months of 2018 would be a reflection on all the good stuff.

Sam was all over the concept of travelling as both hard work and a metaphysical joy when the subject was broached in a conversation with *Heavy Magazine*. "What year is it? Just joking, but yeah it has been crazy. It's been absolutely non-stop for the last two years but it has felt like a lifetime that we've been doing this. It's so busy every day, every day is different. The only thing that is expected is that we don't know what is going to happen next. We get to travel. We get to go around the world, meet fabulous people and have great experiences. I can only compare it to being shot out of a cosmic rocket cannon."

Sam's comments would take on greater significance during the October/November return to Europe. Greta Van Fleet had reached a level of stardom where lot seemed familiar and, in the best possible way, predictable. The band would play their collective asses off. The response would be the same in any language; unbridled enthusiasm. The press would, at each stop, run the gamut from occasionally insightful to primarily pedestrian.

And who was to blame if a certain amount of lethargy would set in. Midway through the 2018 tour, it had pretty much all been said until there was something new to talk about. Greta Van Fleet remained good sports about it all, trotting out pat answers to, in some cases, questions that tried to delve way back in their history. It was no wonder that Dan would say that on some days their whole existence seemed a blur.

"I wish I had more of a memory of what we've been experiencing because, at the moment, it always seems interesting to me. It's always interesting when it's happening now. When you slow down and take the time to write things down, save some of the memories, take pictures or videos, it's good because it is a dream. But now it's becoming so much more personal. It's surreal."

One constant during the later stages of the tour was that the band was always writing new songs. Jake, at odd moments, would be fingering a new riff while Josh would be jotting down new lyrics and presenting them to the rest of the band for their input. Not that there was any rush to get new songs in place. *Anthem of the Peaceful Army* had only been out a few months and there were no hints from the label that it might be time to consider a follow-up album. Being on the move, creatively, was just part and parcel of Greta Van Fleet's DNA.

But at one point during the tour, Sam did concede that the band might have something new up their sleeve.

"We were actually talking about it and we all decided that we needed to do a new album as soon as possible. We're just going to do what we do and we're going to make the music that we want to hear. We've been going places that we've never been before and I think, in a sense, album two will be very worldly. We've been touring the world, having all these new experiences and experiencing all these new sounds. You can't help but having the colors of the mind getting put into a record like this. The one thing I can definitely say right now is that you can expect album two in 2019."

The idea that Greta Van Fleet might be playing in a limited heavy metal pool came to a grinding halt in early December when the very mainstream and not-always hip

Grammy Awards, who once awarded Jethro Tull their heavy metal artist of the year, announced their nominees for the upcoming Grammy Awards ceremony. Greta Van Fleet knew they were infinitely qualified for many of the hard rock categories but they had also been reminded of the organization's often timid attitude when it came to honoring new artists and low-level genres that were suddenly making a comeback. But that did not stop them from being bowled over when the band received Grammy nominations for Best Rock Album (*From the Fires*), Best Rock Song (*"Black Smoke Rising"*), Best Rock Performance (*"Highway Tune")* and Best New Artist.

Greta Van Fleet were blown away by the announcement, acknowledging that getting a Grammy nod was the creative and emotional end to a two year coming-of-age journey. Dan was over the moon when he heard the news and relayed his feelings in a *Grammy.com* interview. "It has been a dream of mine. But for it to happen before 2019 was like having a bucket of water dumped on you to wake you up. It is kind of refreshing and a massive compliment."

Sam, in the same interview, took the news as a sign that the doomsayers who were saying that Greta Van Fleet was plying their trade in a genre that was considered dead were dead wrong. "We know rock is not dead. There's plenty of it out there. That the Grammys nominated a rock band for Best New Artist is the biggest statement that can be made that rock is very much alive."

The 2018 *Anthem of the Peaceful Army* tour would wind down with a three-night stand, December 27-30, at the legendary Fox Theater in Detroit. Very much in the Christmas holiday spirit and a legitimate homecoming celebration for the boys from Frankenmuth, Greta Van

Fleet were the conquering heroes, humbled that the three nights in Detroit would mark the end of a first chapter and the beginning of a second.

2018 had seen the band evolve into a monster of muscular heavy rock band, equal parts swagger and attitude, bent on proving that rock 'n' roll in a live setting was once again an emotional and spiritual experience on a number of levels. The three shows in Detroit easily showed the maturity of the band, the 145-minute set encompassing 13 songs that covered all the bases, from the early songs like "Highway Tune," "Black Smoke Rising" and "Safari Song" to a generous helping of *Anthem of the Peaceful Army*. Greta Van Fleet were exploring, musically and vocally, all the possibilities. There were some surprises during the three nights in Detroit. Honoring one of their early influences, the band offered up the John Denver Song "The Music Is You" and, during what had become a welcome mid-set jam, they served up an enticing bit of the long-ago Melanie classic "Lay Down Candles In The Rain". There could be no doubt that the three shows in Detroit would be gigs for the ages.

Greta Van Fleet would usher in New Year's Eve on the wings of total rock 'n' roll triumph. They had the material and commercial success most bands struggle years to achieve. They had the adulation that most men \in their early 20's could ever dream of getting. And not surprisingly, they were humbled in the face of it all.

Jake said as much when he told *Forbes,* "We're grounded and we're that way by reminding ourselves who we are and where we came from. We're just four young guys who came from a very small town." Likewise, Dan was in the same hometown frame of mind when he told the *Detroit Free Press,* "We come from a very humbling, supportive community. I honestly couldn't be happier (with our success). Where I'm at with my family and these guys. There's nothing to bring me down."

Chapter Twenty-Three

Taking a Hit

Over the decades, *Saturday Night Live* had become the tastemaker in popular culture. A guest shot could turn into a career. Ten minutes in a skit could turn an up-and-comer into a superstar. Especially when it came to the show's choice in musical guests.

By January 2019, Greta Van Fleet had become the hot new kid on the block. They were literally everywhere and were the proverbial must-see. And the notoriety had, not unexpectedly, broken out of the heavy metal milieu into more mainstream arenas to the upwardly mobile millennials with big cars, expensive tastes and eye on what was hip. Pop culture had suddenly perked up its ears. So when *Saturday Night Live* came calling with the offer to be the show's season-opening musical guest, the band would say YES in capital letters.

From a pure business point of view, it seemed to make sense. *Saturday Night Live* had a far-reaching influence on musical tastes that spread far beyond the preconceived notion of Greta Van Fleet's target audience of young, nostalgic rockers. But the band was not really thinking that way. For Greta Van Fleet it was all about memories.

"*Saturday Night Live* is just another one of those things that has come full circle for us," Sam told *Vulture.com*. "We used to watch *Saturday Night Live* growing up as a family when we couldn't sleep. It's a recircling of something very relevant. *Saturday Night Live* is one of those milestones."

And on Saturday night, January 19, the band went live in front of millions of television viewers. The results would be decidedly mixed. Greta Van Fleet would play two songs, "Black Smoke Rising" and "You're The One" amidst the crowded studio set that, from the outset, seemed somewhat intimidating to the already nervous band.

There was also the question of a sound system that fell short of the requirements of a loud, live rock band. Both seemed much in evidence on "'Black Smoke Rising." The band threw everything into the song and, on occasion, played with true fire but, for the most part, appeared swallowed up by the logistics of the television set up. "You're The One" showed the band to be a bit more comfortable, but not much.

Die-hard fans, in the Twitter storm that followed the performance, were charitable, but even they had to admit that it was not Greta Van Fleet's finest moment. And theories would fall like raindrops as to why Greta Van Fleet was being slammed for their *Saturday Night Live* appearance. Some put the blame on too much touring and not enough rest. Others cited the pressures of working on a new album as the culprit. Still others blamed the less-than-stellar response to *Anthem of a Peaceful Army*, and in particular, the slam job courtesy of *Pitchfork*, for hurting their creative feelings.

Greta Van Fleet tour manager Michael Barbee, who always seemed ready for an "out there" response to any

136

question, told *Alternative Nation.com* that *"Saturday Night Live* happened way too soon. I don't think they were remotely ready for that. *Saturday Night Live* should have waited another year. It just didn't go well. It's a lot to take in for being young guys. They had just dropped an album; everyone was cramming them and now they're on *Saturday Night Live*. It's a lot to take in."

As to what the band thought of the criticism, Sam proved to have the thickest skin when it came to addressing the media. He would tell *Kill Your Stereo.com* "We really thought that it was a great performance. There's a certain amount of television and audio that can get messed up in the mix. Rock 'n' roll is not perfect. The thing is that it was a performance. The way we do our music is, inherently, a little sloppy. Creativity is not always pretty.

"We play real music and what happened with *Saturday Night Live* is what happens when you play real music."

Chapter Twenty-Four

Say Hello to 2019

Greta Van Fleet took the month of January 2019 off. At least on the surface it seemed that way.

But the reality was that the press was always calling and there continued to be a lot to talk about. The 2019 leg of the *Anthem of the Peaceful Army* was scheduled to kick off in February and run through much of the year. Their four Grammy nominations would also continue to interest the world. There had been preliminary talk about the band performing live on the Grammys but it was still up in the air, owing to the logistics of the 2019 schedule. But the band was also quick to point out that while they were finding moments to hang with friends and visit old haunts, creatively they were still firing on all cylinders.

"Once we finished the final mix on *Anthem of the Peaceful Army*, the very next day we started writing the next album," Jake told *The Associated Press*. "If we're stagnant, it becomes boring."

The band knew they would never completely shake the Led Zeppelin comparison and had, by this time, given up hope that they ever would. But they were doing their best to put the emphasis elsewhere. They were already laying down some preliminary demos on new material as time allowed and, as Josh offered to *Rolling Stone,* progress on new material was being made. "We're definitely setting some groundwork for the next album which we're hoping to get out sometime this year. We're feeling less pressure than we were on the last album. We can't wait to explore a little more of the Greta Van Fleet universe."

The first phase of the 2019 tour would be a mammoth international undertaking, encompassing 10 international countries, including shows in Spain, Germany, Paris and a five-show stint in the UK between January 29 and March 15. But the tour would get off to a bumpy start. The buzz that Greta Van Fleet would most certainly receive one if not more Grammy awards had the band canceling an appearance in New Zealand so they could be in Los Angeles to participate in the festivities. A long-anticipated three-show kickoff in Australia would also have to be cancelled at the last possible moment when Josh fell victim to a rock singer's malady, as he would later disclose in a *Facebook* message.

"Somewhere between travel from the US to Japan and Australia I developed an upper respiratory infection that gradually evolved into laryngitis. I've been trying to recover but cannot seem to get rid of it. Doctors have informed me that performing in this condition could cause damage to my vocal cords, which is something that I cannot risk and therefore we must reschedule our shows."

The band did get it together to go to Los Angeles for The Grammy Awards but, as the plane carrying the band touched down in Los Angeles, a lot of questions and a bit of controversy surrounding the ceremony continued to circle them.

It remained up in the air whether or not Greta Van Fleet would perform on the televised show. Ultimately the decision was made that they would not perform, with many pundits chalking up the decision to both Josh's throat issues and the conservative thinking on the part of the Academy when it came to offering too much time to the coming new wave of rock at the expense of the reigning music forms of pop and hip-hop. Further fuel to the fire was the fact that the rock awards would be regulated to a secondary awards program prior to the televised main show. While the Academy would do their best to justify their decisions, the rock community was, to a large degree, up in arms at the perceived slight.

Speculation was running wild as to how well Greta Van Fleet would do. Stories in the media were wildly speculating everything from a clean sweep of their four nominations to maybe two at best. The band did their best to avoid the speculation of their own, but Jake would add his two cents in conversation with *The Associated Press*. "I think Best Album and Best Performance would be some of the more highlighted categories I'd like us to win. It seems to me that Best New Artist is sort of a cursed category. But if we get it, we'll accept it."

But as it turned out, when Greta Van Fleet's one Grammy victory, Best Rock Album for *From the Fires*, was announced during the largely untelevised portion of the ceremony, not one member of Greta Van Fleet came to the stage to accept the award. The reason why was never really explained. But the band was highly visible during an energetic two-song set at a post-Grammy party.

Playing that party may not have been the best idea because, mere days after the performance, Josh had a relapse of his throat ailment. It was shortly before Greta Van Fleet were scheduled to fly to Europe to kick off the 2019 tour. The band decided to cancel the European shows.

In a *Facebook* message, the band revealed their decision. "A year and a half of constant touring has been both invigorating and exhausting. Josh currently has a relentless upper respiratory infection that has not yet had a chance to heal. His doctor has required extensive rest. It now feels necessary for the entire band to recalibrate our balance both physically and mentally rather than continuing on with more performances and exacerbate things further."

The reasoning seemed overly dramatic and a bit wordy, but the bottom line reality was clear. Greta Van Fleet needed a bit of R and R. But the band could not be sedentary too long and word began to leak out that Greta Van Fleet were now in full on writing mode. The band would make its return to touring on March 28 at the Lollapalooza Festival in Chile. There was both excitement and trepidation in the air as Greta Van Fleet took the stage. Word was that Josh was now fully recovered but it would be this performance that would tell the tale.

The consensus during the band's 10-song set was that Josh had truly recovered, his soaring, emotional vocals hitting those trademark octaves with ease. The songs were a bit of a departure from a predictable set list. Trademark fan favorites "Black Smoke Rising" and "Safari Song" went down well as did a tantalizing mixture of newer material. In a progressive aside, Greta Van Fleet delivered an expansive cover of the song "Watch Me"' by British poet, songwriter and essayist Labi Siffre, which the band had played for the first time in a November 2018 concert in the UK. The time off had definitely done the band some good and primed the performing pump for Greta Van Fleet's return to the North American portion of the tour, kicking off with a May 7 show in Miami.

It was during the early months of 2019 that one of

the more intriguing announcements surrounding the band was made. A planned 50th anniversary celebration in honor of the original Woodstock Festival was announced and the initial lineup included both Greta Van Fleet and Robert Plant. The rock world was on fire with the notion that a member of Led Zeppelin, the band's primary influence, might be sharing the stage with his musical offspring. Would they do a song together? But at that point nothing was being announced about a cross generational mash-up.

But by that time, it was too late. The internet was alive with speculation of a Led Zeppelin/Greta Van Fleet meeting in some form. And tour manager Michael Barbee was not above stirring the pot when he told *Alternative Nation.com* his theory. "If Josh stepped in as a singer for Led Zeppelin he would nail it and do a great job. But I don't know what point it would make for Josh to be a guest singer for Zeppelin because that would just be feeding the frenzy."

The next six weeks saw the band crisscrossing a good part of the United States and Canada, and the full impact of their sudden stardom remained much in evidence. Larger venues, sold-out shows, added dates, spectacular reviews were constant reminders that Greta Van Fleet had truly risen from the ashes of a long-dormant musical genre to once again capture the essence of what it was to rock heavy and true. But unbeknownst to the legions of fans was the fact that the band was finding time amid the madness of celebrity to enter a Los Angeles studio to create new music with a brand-new producer.

But by July, the cat would be out of the bag. As reported by the *Detroit Free Press*, *Alternative Nation.com*, *Loudwire* and a host of other media outlets, the band had been secretly working with the new hot producer on the block Greg Kurstin. Kurstin had come to his success thanks to a string of credits that included Adele, Kelly Clarkson, Paul McCartney, Pink, Beck, The Foo Fighters and Kendrik Lamar. Reportedly sharp as a tack when it came to different styles of music and a willingness to take any genre to that next step, Kurstin, nevertheless, would seem an odd choice to pilot Greta Van Fleet's next album.

Doubters pointed to the fact that many of Kirstin's credits were blatantly pop in nature and seemingly far removed from the sensibilities of hard rock. There would be many theories as to this "out of left field" choice. Record label influence? Perhaps, as Kirstin's many credits also included fellow Lava Records artist Lorde. Nobody could argue with the commercial success of *Anthem of the Peaceful Army,* but there had been speculation that the label was looking for a different sound that might be more radio-friendly. How much of the decision was the band's was also a consideration. It was evident that after two successful EP's and a full- length album, the band was still unable to escape the Led Zeppelin comparisons and was looking for a chance of direction that might silence the critics for good.

In an interview with *New Musical Express* shortly before the news broke, Jake and Sam were upfront in saying that, sound-wise, it might be time for a change. "The new music we're working on is definitely much different than the music on *Anthem of the Peaceful Army*," said Jake. "We have more leniency on the more outlandish stuff we want to do," Sam added, "The new music is a step in a cinematic direction." Sam further indicated to *Billboard* that the lineup was "doing a lot more writing, getting some stuff recorded and we've started working on the next thing."

But it would remain for Jake to tell *NME* that, in no uncertain terms, the band was pulling out all the stops in a not-too-veiled attempt at finally distancing themselves from the Led Zeppelin albatross. "When it comes to this album I suppose the question is what hasn't been done and how many rules can we break? Because when it gets to that point, you really start creating something unique."

There would be news aplenty during August. It was announced that Greta Van Fleet would open for Metallica during the South American leg of their 2020 world tour. Fans would also be disappointed to discover that the Woodstock 50 event that would, in their minds, feature the clash of the heavy metal titans in Greta Van Fleet and Robert Plant, had run afoul of a myriad of financial and logistical problems and had finally been cancelled.

But there was speculation surrounding Greta Van Fleet's reported new album. Jason Flom, the head of Lava Records, was quick to prime the pump when he stated by way of an interview transcript in *Alternative Nation*.com that, "Last night I got a sneak preview of some amazing new music that my favorite band Greta Van Fleet are making."

It would be reported—more speculation than anything else—that the band would be going into the studio in October and that an album would be rush-released before the end of the year, which renewed speculation then deemed would most likely be released early in 2020.

Between September and November, Greta Van Fleet would be riding high on both the national and international concert trail. The vibe surrounding the band was now something akin to rock royalty. Considered rock 'n' roll nomads because of their extensive touring, the band had now evolved in the public's eye as more worldly and sophisticated rock troubadours. They were confident in their live performing universe, moving easily through the perks and privilege of rock stardom.

They were allowing the slings and arrows of critics to become simply another element of the white noise that served as background to the moment in their lives.

That the band was remaining pure in the face of it all was a whole other matter. Backstage photos showing the band surrounded by bottles of alcohol indicated that certain temptations were inevitable. But the presence of smart adults around them was proving the stumbling block to access. Greta Van Fleet were constantly on the road, in and out of the studio working on their new album and, just too damned busy making music to get into any trouble.

Most notable was the cult of personality and influence that had sprung up around the band. There was less of an aura of gimmickry and PR flackery and more of a sense that, musically, Greta Van Fleet were ushering in a new generation that wanted to follow in their footsteps. Jake would address that point in an interview with *Metalhead Zone.com*. "We've always been aware that we were going to be influential, mainly to young musicians. That seems to be the chain or evolution of how music works and will always work."

Chapter Twenty-Five

Time Has Come

Greta Van Fleet had their fans foaming at the mouth at the prospect of new music by the end of 2019. And by September 2019, they would make good on their tease. Sort of. The band announced that the song "Always There," which had been recorded during the *Anthem of the Peaceful Army* sessions but not included in the album, was released as part of the soundtrack for the movie *A Million Little Pieces*, in theaters in December.

The band's popularity would continue to resonate with other elements of media during 2019. Their song "When The Curtain Falls" was in an episode of the television series *Magnum P.I.,* while the songs "Black Smoke Rising" and "Edge Of Darkness" were used in the one-season online techno thriller series *Project EVE*.

It was about this time when rumors began to fly that at least two members of Greta Van Fleet were in some semblance of a relationship. As reported in *Alternative Nation.com*, Josh was seeing a girl on a regular basis, and Dan had a steady girlfriend who would occasionally join him on the road. Alternately believable and unbelievable, this bit of Greta Van Fleet titillation would disappear after an extremely short shelf life.

Because, truth be told, there really was not a lot of time in Greta Van Fleet's world for a personal life.

September through October saw Greta Van Fleet in consummate road warrior mode, hitting both US and international dates in a methodical, yet always entertaining spectacle of a rock 'n' roll experience. And it was a tour that constantly reinforced the fact that, despite their youth, Greta Van Fleet had matured into a cohesive and highly personal unit that has not crumbled under the pressures of the road. It was a subject that Jake considered in conversation with *The Florida Times Union.*

"Touring has its moments and it can be a blessing and a curse," he conceded. "But it never seems to get too personal. We have a level of respect for each other. We're out traveling across the world and you have to rely on each other to keep each other in check." In the same conversation, Jake described long distance touring as an ever-changing world. "Sometimes the language is Portuguese or Japanese. But the only thing that doesn't change is the moment when we get on stage. That remains the same all over the world. When it comes to the music, it's a constant evolution. It seems that growth and change occur organically."

While the road had become a literal home away from home for Greta Van Fleet, it was also something that pulled the band away from their growing second love, the recording studio. The band was continuing to make time to track for the by-now much-anticipated next album, but, in conversation with Blabbermouth.net, Sam emphasized that the recording process was being conducted in fits and starts. "We've been kind of in and out of the studio. We've been doing so much touring lately that we've kind of had to back out. It's always difficult to find time to get into the studio, record and get into that mindset. But 2019 will definitely include a lot of studio time."

Greta Van Fleet's last official act of 2019 would be November 26. at the Saint Jordi Club in Barcelona, Spain. The last leg of the 2019 tour had been pretty much like the previous months on the road: physically and emotionally demanding. The highs of taking their music to the people from every part of the world met the fatigue connected to celebrity. For Greta Van Fleet it was a battle that ultimately ended in the triumph thanks in no small part to the adrenaline rush of making it to the top.

Now it was time to go home.

But Greta Van Fleet was far from finished.

For the next five months they would continue in the whirlwind. There would be precious time away from the spotlight where they could, at least for a while, once again be the four guys from Frankenmuth. Plus, a lot of time in the studio, crafting a new album. In fact, from August through September, the band was in and out of a Los Angeles studio quite a bit, as Jake reported to the *Orange County Register*. "We've had a month off the road and we've spent it recording and seeing what would happen. We didn't come in with any predisposed ideas of what would come of it. But we had a variety of different songs and things so we knew what we wanted to accomplish. What came out of all of it was quite interesting and that makes it exciting."

Already preparing for a 2020 tour that would kick off in April with the much-anticipated South American tour with Metallica in Chile, Argentina and Brazil, the band was literally salivating at the prospect at entering yet-another uncharted musical universe. "We do like Metallica," Jake gushed to the *Pasadena Star News*. "We kind of figured they would be the perfect group to go down to South America with. I can't even imagine what experiences lay ahead. We just know the audiences down there are absolutely wild. So I think that will be a true adventure."

Much beyond that was still vague with the exception of a projected July 4 festival date in Poland. But the band was confident that a mammoth slate of US and international dates would most certainly fill out. Because when you reach that plateau that Greta Van Fleet has ascended to, the world of rock 'n' roll tends to take care of itself.

For Greta Van Fleet, the journey has been a rock 'n' roll fairy tale that has turned out to have one big happy ending. But the band is not resting on their laurels. They know what they want for the future, and exactly what they have to do to make the magic.

It all boils down to hard work. But then again, that's always been what Greta Van Fleet is all about.

Chapter Twenty-Six

Can You Top This?

Greta Van Fleet were nothing if not quick learners. Their first studio album, *Anthem of a Peaceful Army* touched down in October 2018, The band, emotionally and otherwise, was already chomping at the bit for round two. Which would be quite the accomplishment considering their debut studio effort *Anthem of a Peaceful Army* had been nothing short of a heavy metal miracle.

Anthem of a Peaceful Army, upon its release in October 2018, was an immediate hit with the first two singles out of the box, 'When The Curtain Falls' and 'You're The One' effectively priming the singles chart pump and setting the stage for *Anthem of a Peaceful Army* to debut at No. 3 on the *Billboard* album charts. Critically, the band continued to have its naysayers amid the prickling Led Zeppelin comparisons and Greta Van Fleet's youth and obvious influences. But where it counted, to the legion of fans that bought the albums and flocked to the band's concerts, Greta Van Fleet were monsters of the reemerging of the hard rock and heavy metal scene.

Proof positive of the band's popularity was the accounting of *Concert Archives.com* which listed Greta Van Fleet's concert appearances between 217-220 at just a shade under 300 gigs including, most notably, a pair of gigs opening for Metallica in South America. In hindsight, going on the road would translate into a lot of on-the-job training and influence in their upcoming recording projects according to a *Rolling Stone* conversation with drummer Danny Wagner and guitarist Jake Kiszka. Wagner acknowledged "We realized that growing up we had been shielded from a lot of things and then we were thrown out into this huge world. It was a bit of a culture shock at first." Kiszka would elaborate "The more we've seen, the different cultures, people and traditions, made us realize how similar we all are."

Greta Van Fleet would crash out *The Battle at Garden's Gate* literally moments after the completion of *Anthem of a Peaceful Army*. And that recording burn, coupled with sporadic touring to finish out 2019 and into 2020, made the members of the band alternately leery and upfront about what was to come with the by now much anticipated *The Battle at Garden's Gate*.

Josh, in conversation with *Kerrang!*, was a tad on the cautious side as he danced around what to expect on *The Battle at Garden's Gate*. "The new album is intended to be a full release, a full album. We really poured everything into the writing. We felt we had something to prove. We make music for somebody who has a reason to listen to it. We're creating something simply for the sake of making a work of art."

Back on the road after the completion of *The Battle at Garden's Gate* and dealing with a new rush of international interest, brothers Jake and Sam opened up a tad on what to expect. Sam explored what was to come with *New Musical Express* when he used words like "sonic" and 'other worldly." We're incorporating more sounds, more tones

152

and more new styles of music." Jake dotted the descriptive, when he offered, "We're doing with this album what hasn't been done before and we're seeing how many rules we can break. Quite simply, we're doing something completely different."

A sense of what that 'something different' would be became evident when a new song "My Way Home," complete with a band-directed video was released in October 2020, a full seven months before the April 2021 release of the album. Over the early months of the album, the band would release what were in essence new singles ''Age Of Machine," "Heat Above" and "Broken Bells" to keep Greta Van Fleet in the public eye. The plan worked as *The Battle at Garden's Gate* crashed all international rock and metal charts, including top ten on *Billboard*.

But, in the classic rock and roll sense, Greta Van fleet were nowhere to be found. Unless one booked their international touring itinerary well in advance."

Chapter Twenty-Seven

On The Road Again

It seemed like only yesterday that Greta Van Fleet had been on the road for any prolonged period of time. But the reality was that by the time the band had essentially completed *Anthem of a Peaceful Army* and *The Battle at Garden's Gate* back to back, they had been studio-bound for a reported 27 months that included time off because of the Covid epidemic and the reality that what had started off as more fun and games than a career had over a period of time morphed into a band on the verge of real life rock and roll superstardom. Some decisions had to be made and the first was to pack up and move to Nashville for their permanent base of operations.

Sam offered how the decision came to pass in a conversation with *The Tennessean*. "We had no real reason to settle down but, because of the whole Covid thing, we were forced to stop, recollect and understand who we are in this world other than just musicians. Suddenly it was perspective forcing us. Daniel and I were living in Los Angeles and we realized that this wasn't going to brush over. We knew that what we were up to was something serious and so we all decided to headquarters out of Nashville. Everything is here, all our friends, musicians and artists. It makes it really easy to work now and there's a lot of art to be made."

Late in February 1922, the band took its first tentative step back on the road when they opened a pair of shows for Metallica in Las Vegas, Nevada. Surprisingly there was not a whole lot they had to relearn. They hadn't forgotten a thing, their timing was spot on and their newer material went down quite well.

But to say that the band still needed to tune up their road jones was an understatement. Because Greta Van Fleet, four years on, had evolved into quite the perfectionists.

Hence *The Strange Tour*, a shakedown tour of minimal proportions. 14 shows encompassing stops in Tennessee, Connecticut, Illinois, Texas, Los Angeles and Georgia, the better to fine-tune a set list and to play around with stage presence and choreography. By the end of 2021, the rust had been shaken off and the band was ready for the big show.

The big show being the *Dream of Gold* tour which would take Greta Van Fleet on a North American coming out party of headlining arena shows to celebrate the success of *The Battle at Garden's Gate* and as well as the unofficial arrival of Greta Van Fleet as certified superstars.

But shortly after the *Dream of Gold tour* was scheduled to begin, with a five-date series of shows for old times' sake in Michigan, fate would unexpectedly step in to throw the band a curve ball. As chronicled in *Blabbermmouth.net* and countless other websites, announced that concerts in Flint and Ypsilanti were postponed after Josh and Jake fell ill. It was determined that it was not Covid and that the band was set to reschedule the remainder of the tour when, on

March 16, six days into the start of the *Dream of Gold* tour, that guitarist Jake Kiszka had fallen victim to pneumonia and had been hospitalized, effectively cancelling a show in *West Virginia*.

The band promptly released several public statements, explaining in positive terms how Jake was on the road to recovery and that the band would reschedule all the cancelled performances and that they hoped their fans would understand. The reality was that, according to Sam in conversation with *USA Today*, the situation was much more dire than Greta Van Fleet was letting on.

"The situation was much worse than many fans initially realized," he revealed. "Jake was actually close to losing a lung."

An object lesson being that even rock stars get sick. Jake eventually recovered and Greta Van Fleet continued on through May. The first leg of the *Dream of Gold* tour would play out in a European and South American series of shows that included opening acts for Metallica in Brazil, Chile and Argentina and headlining gigs in Mexico, Sweden, France, Germany, Ireland and the UK. Upon returning back to the states they discovered that the first leg of the *Dream of Gold* tour had been a complete sellout and that promoters were falling all over themselves for a second leg of the US tour. But Sam was quick to note that Jake's illness had forced the band to recreate the remainder of the tour on the fly as well as to rethink how they would handle the strenuous pace of a tour from that point forward.

"We were hustling to create a different show as we went along," he told *USA Today*. "It became kind of a skeleton show to try and get through it. We talked about show openers Rival Sons merging with our set to take some pressure off Jake. We realized that from now on touring would have to be about pacing ourselves. It became about knowing what we could take, what we could do and what we would be able to pull off on the road."

That attitude melded into a philosophical aside to Greta Van Fleet's next album entitled *Starchaser*. The reality was that the band had been working on bits and pieces of the album since 2021. They had material but Sam acknowledged in *USA Today* that they still had questions.

"What do we do now? We've just reached the mountaintop. Where do we go from here?"

Chapter Twenty-Eight

Starcatcher Raw

If you stick a needle in most guitarists, the chances are good that you're going to find a deep thinker at the core. One year removed from dealing with pneumonia, a monster, career defining breakthrough album in *The Battle at Garden's Gate* and a *Dream of Gold* tour that seemed to go on forever, and it seemed that guitarist Jake Kiszka was spot on when it came to being a deep thinking cat.

It became evident in conversation with *Cleveland. com* that Kiszka, emotionally and psychologically, was fully capable of venturing deep inside. "When we're crafting a record or writing individual songs, it doesn't necessarily appear to me that it is something that is going to touch people or affect people or change people. But we've been able to see that over the last year. There's been a symbolic quality associated with each song, that's the way it's been received. It's quite elating. We're very thought out and premeditated in what we do. For us, I think that's part of telling a story. We've found that, for us, there's a point where you can go too far."

Consequently, post *Dream of Gold*, the members of Greta Van Fleet could be forgiven if mentally, emotionally and creatively they were all over the place.

They were making the occasional trips back to Frankenmuth to reconnect with friends, places and everything that was part and parcel of their world before their world changed forever. Back in Nashville, it was rest, relaxation and going over their previous album and what would change in their next album, *Starcatcher*. There would be firsts. Recording in and around Georgia and Nashville, a new producer, Dave Cobb, and striving to get away from the concept of cinematic and sonic that marked *The Battle at Garden's Gate*.

In a conversation with *USA Today*, Sam fondly recalled what worked on their last album but was just as quickly anxious to move on to songs like "Meeting The Master," "The Falling Sky" and "Farewell For Now." For his part, drummer Wagner, talking to *New Musical Express*, was more literal in the game plan for *Starcatcher*. "We had this idea that we wanted to tell these stories, to build a universe. We wanted to introduce ideas that would come about here and there, throughout our careers through this world."

Sam was more to the point, exacting in detail, in *USA Today* and *Vogue* the nuts and bolts of the band returning to the nostalgic/creative days of yesteryear. "We were going for a more raw sound that we used on the early albums. After *The Battle at Garden's Gate*, it was difficult to say what the next move was. The obvious move to me was to look back and say 'okay, let's layer this one all up with string parts, orchestration sections and thousands of overdubs, let's just make every part count.' With *Starcatcher* we just decided to minimize and maximize the sound. The way the harmony worked just made it all big and powerful It was a lot more than just doing a lot of guitar parts.

160

"One of our main goals for *Starcatcher* was to create something candid, exciting and authentic. It is likely the least preconceived album we've ever put together A lot of the things were happening and recorded happened on the final take only once."

Long story short, Greta Van Fleet's largely back to the future approach seemed to work. Coupled with the staggered release of songs from the album brought advance positive notice that translated into instant chart success upon its July 23, 2023 release. The hoopla and hype were expected.

Until one member of the band dropped a bombshell.

Chapter Twenty-Nine

Josh Has Something to Say

Going into late June 2023 and Josh Kiszka was right in the middle of a lot of hard work. There was yet another round of pre-release hype on *Starcatcher* to contend with. There was also a mammoth world tour that was most certainly going to dwarf anything Greta Van Fleet had accomplished to that point.

But on June 20, 2023, Josh decided that easily the most important thing he had ever done was more important and he was going to tell the world about it. On Tuesday June 20, 2023, Josh Kiszka came out to millions of people as a gay man.

In an *Instagram* announcement carried by the likes of *Rolling Stone*, *Billboard*, *Pink News*, *Out Magazine* and, yes, even *The Huron Daily Tribune*, Josh stated "I am in a loving, same-sex relationship with my partner for the past eight years."

Not surprisingly, the response to Josh's announcement ran the gamut of emotions, disbelief by Greta Van Fleet fans at large and support from those in his inner circle. His brother Jake was one of the first to weigh in in conversation with *Guitar.com*. "I'm proud of him but I think, more so, I'm in awe of his bravery, his compassion and the amount of power that he holds. It's one thing to explain your sexual orientation to someone close or in your family. But when you go to announce something like that to millions and the world, you're sort of standing naked before God and his mighty men saying, 'Here I am. Take it or leave it.' I think it's great. I think it's time. I think he was ready."

Speculation aside, there was several indications, over the years about what Josh's sexual orientation might be. Little, if anything, was known about the band's personal life, a subject that was perceived to be off limits to the public. For his part, Josh's flamboyant stage costumes, ala early period David Bowie, hinted at certain proclivities in his private life. Most recently, the overriding themes of *Starcatcher* whose overriding theme was the search for freedom and identity made Josh's feelings fairly obvious. In further extracts from his *Instagram* announcement excerpted in the *Huron Daily Tribune* and *Billboard*, Josh reflected on what brought him to coming out.

"When I moved to Nashville in 2020m, I found myself right in the middle of culture wars by Tennessee legislators were proposing bills that would threaten the freedom of love. Ultimately when enough injustice happens you can't just stand by and watch it happen any longer. I didn't want kids that are part of the LBGTQ community to feel that they should be victims or that they should be frightened. I felt that it was imperative that I speak my truth for not only for myself but in hopes of changing hearts, minds and laws in Tennessee and beyond."

But as Greta Van Fleet began to gear up for the start of the *Starcatcher* tour which would kick off in Nashville in July, Josh's positivity was momentarily replaced by a moment of doubt as he recalled in *Rolling Stone*. "I was afraid that I would end up having a target on my back." But the moment of doubt would quickly be replaced by a note of confidence. "Everything would be met with love and acceptance and humility and respect. For me, that was a huge wave of reassurance that things were going in the right direction. As a performer and as an entertainer a huge weight was lifted off my shoulders because, as an artist and as a person, we all want to be understood."

Josh's hopes and, yes, fears were put to the test on the stage when Greta Van Fleet stepped on the stage in front of a sold-out crowd in Nashville. At one point in the concert Josh looked out into a sea of fans who were holding up colored pieces of paper configured into the shape of a rainbow. The spectacle told Josh everything he needed to know.

"Emotionally it was really difficult to keep it together."

Chapter Thirty

Planning and Downtime

The logistics of *The Greta Van Fleet World Tour* were a massive undertaking... Even before the band would kick off the first date of a tour that would run through the end of 2024. The odds that the band will manage some time off to record a new album or two seemed certain. But new music aside., this is the way the tour was slated to unfold.

July 24, 2023. Nonstop shows through January 20, 2024. Then a month off for good behavior and back on the road beginning February 23 and on into the future. Where hard work knows no limits.

In conversation with *USA Today*, some time before the start of the *Starcatcher World Tour*, Sam outlined the plans for the road. "I think a very strong theme on the *Starcatcher World Tour* is going to be *The Falling Sky*. It's going to be the quintessential Greta Van Fleet. It's going to be all-encompassing as far as the new album goes. We'll also be bringing back some really old tunes. Remembering a bit will be important to us. We have a lot of songs now. The shows will be really about connecting with the people who know all the songs who really want to hear those things."

Flash forward to January 2024. Greta Van Fleet are

taking a well-earned break at home in Nashville. Superstar rockers with too much time on their hands? One can only cringe as the tabloids wring their hands, waiting for the other show to drop. And one would be disappointed that, light years removed from the chaos caused by Led Zeppelin (there you knew that comparison was coming) it would be a very sedate Sam Kyszka who enlightens *Spin.com* of some of the not so gory details.

"All of this is still considered alien to me," he confessed. "I'm still trying to learn what to make of it all. I'm trying to find shit to do right now."

Upon further examination Sam reflects on his life off the road in much the same manner as the rest of the band. There's the occasional sense of longing and nostalgia at the way it used to be. But he is quick to point out "that it's all so different now." The band's downtime is not much different than it is when trying to find a quiet moment on the road or in the studio when his mind is never far from what the band has accomplished and what they are truly capable of. He reportedly has used his downtime to write songs and entertain the notion of producing other artists (which at publication time remains vague).

Sam does like the isolation and the privacy. He's big on meditation and quiet walks in the woods. He likes to kayak, works in the garden. As with the other members of the band, there's a constant sense of restlessness that drives Sam. On a whim, he once jumped in his car and drove and just drove to North Carolina. In a bit of understatement, he described the excuse of this spontaneous trip as part and parcel of the makeup of Greta Van Fleet.

"It's hard to be off the road and not see new places and things every day." He offered *Spin.com*. "It comes from a place of hoping that we can do our absolute best and work on our absolute highest level all the time." And it would be an attitude that would follow the members of Greta Van Fleet well into February 2024. As instinct set in as the very attitudes that propelled the band in concert were a regular visitor to their time off, as explained by Sam in Spin.com.

"The nighttime is really a great time for just being inspired as an artist," he said. "Once the sun sets it's like reality has just kind of faded away and you can live in this fiction-oriented world that you created. That's when I start getting urges to sit down at the piano. I start thinking of interesting things, sit down at the computer and start recording this kind of stuff. Or one of the other guys will have an idea and say 'come on over here really quick and then we'll lay down a demo for this track.' "

Driven as they are, the band's downtime and moments of creative inspiration continue to run in meditative hand in hand. But by mid-February, Greta Van Fleet saw and felt the signals. For each member, it was time to pack the 40-plus bags of equipment and stage-performing gear. *Starcatcher* was setting the critical and commercial world on fire but, for the band, it was, quite simply a sign to hit the road where the rest of 2024 was waiting.

For Greta Van Fleet the hard work that got them to the top was waiting. And where hard work would be their just rewards.

Addendum

Robert Plant Has Something To Say

Legendary singer Robert Plant has a way about him. He can either come across as serious business, tongue -in-cheek or downright dismissive. Of the latter frame of mind, he once dismissed White Snake singer David Coverdale as David Coverversion. With the inception of Greta Van Fleet and their very Plant-sounding Josh Kiszka, what he thinks of the kids from Detroit has evolved into a snark fest, as chron-icled by the likes of the *Detroit Free Press, Loudwire.com, Blabbermouth.net, LEO Weekly* and any music publications worth the guts to broach Plant with the GVF question. What follows is a sampling of the Zeppelin singer's snappiest comebacks.

"They are Led Zeppelin 1.
"Josh Kiszka is a beautiful little singer."
"I hate him."
"He's got a huge voice and he borrowed it from somebody I know very well. But what are you going to do? That's okay."
"Yeah. Those guys from Detroit."
"The singer is pretty good. There's a job somewhere for him."

The members of the band would be diplomatic at every opportunity. Josh, who had been the primary target of Plant's tongue-in-cheek barbs put it this way. "Robert Plant is the world's greatest rock vocalist."

APPENDIX

DISCOGRAPHY

ALBUMS

ANTHEM OF THE PEACEFUL ARMY
(October 19, 2018)

Songs: "Age of Man," "The Cold Wind," "When The Curtain Falls," "Watching Over," "Lover Leaver Taker Believer," "You're The One," "The New Day, Mountain of the Sun," "Brave New World," "Anthem."

FROM THE FIRES
(November 10, 2017)

Songs: "Safari Song," "Edge of Darkness," "Flower Power," "A Change is Gonna Come," "Highway Tune," "Meet on the Ledge," "Talk on the Street," "Black Smoke Rising."

BLACK SMOKE RISING
(April 21, 2017)

Songs: "Highway Tune," "Safari Song," "Flower Power," "Black Smoke Rising."

GRETA VAN FLEET: LIVE IN DETROIT
(2014)

Songs: "Highway Tune," "Cloud Train," "Lover Leaver Taker Believer," "Standing On," "Written in Gold."

HE BATTLE AT GARDEN'S GATE
(Released April 19, 2021)

Songs: "Heat Above," "My Way Soon," "Broken Belts," "Built By Nations," "Age of Machine," "Tears of Rain," "Stardust Chords," "Caravel," "The Barbarians," "Trip The Light Fantastic," "The Weight of Dreams"

STARCATCHER
(Released July 21, 2023)

Songs: "Fate of The Faithful," "Waited All Your Life," "The Falling Sky," "Sacred The Thread," "Runway Blues," "The Indigo Streak," "Frozen Light," "The Archer," "Meeting The Master," "Farewell For Now"

SINGLES

(2019)

"Lover Leaver Taker Believer"

(2017)

"Highway Tune," "Safari Song"

(2018)

"When The Curtain Falls," "You're The One," "Anthem"

(2020)

"My Way Soon" (Oct. 9, 2020)
"Age of Machine" (Dec. 4, 2020)

(2021)
"Heat Above" (Feb. 10, 2021)
" Broken Belts" (Feb. 19, 2021)
"Built By Nations" (April 16, 2021)

(2023)
"Meeting The Master" (April 7, 2023)
Sacred The Thread" (May 19, 2023)
 "Farewell For Now" (June 19, 2023)
"The Falling Sky" (June 27, 2023)

COMPLETE RECORDINGS LIST

What follows is the complete and often-obscure list of recordings made by the band other than the official albums and EP's. These include outtakes from recording sessions, live garage recordings, live concert recordings and recordings of original songs that, to date, have never been released in any form. Bootlegs are out there, but not included. Some recordings are readily available, while some are literally impossible to find. Happy hunting. A great big thanks to Lama Renegade for doing the grunt work and making it public.

(2012)
"Vagabond" (garage recording), "By The River Side" (garage recording), "House of the Rising Sun" (live recording), "Crazy Train" (live recording)

(2013)
"Highway Tune" (limited edition promotional copy)
"Standing On" (garage recording)

(2014)
OUTTAKES FROM THE LIVE IN DETROIT SESSION

"Down To The River," "Lover Leaver Taker Believe Her" (early version before song title change), "Safari Song," "Sing In The Rain," "Thunder Stomp," "You're the One" (early version).

NON LIVE IN DETROIT RECORDINGS

"Flower Power," "I Wanna Be Her Man" (Led Zeppelin cover).

(2015)

"Talk," "The Open C Song," "Morning Maiden," "The Beauty in It," "The Ocean" (live Led Zeppelin cover), "Immigrant Song" (live Led Zeppelin cover), "Whole Lotta Love" (live Led Zeppelin cover), "San Francisco" (live Scott McKenzie cover).

(2016)

"Get You Down" (live)

(2017)

"Mountain of the Sun" (live), "Watching Over" (live), "When the Cold Wind Blows" (live), "I'm the One" (live Howlin' Wolf song), "Stompin' All Down" (live John Lee Hooker song), "That's All Right" (live Arthur Crudup song), "Evil" (live Howlin' Wolf song), "Blueberry Hill" (live Fats Domino song), "Roadhouse Blues" (live Doors song).

(2018)

"Killing Floor" (live Howlin' Wolf song), "Maggie McGill" (live Doors song featuring the Kiska's dad),

"Saturday Night's Alright For Fighting" (live with Elton John), "Hey Jude" (live Beatles song with The Cloves).

SOUNDTRACK CONTRIBUTIONS

(2016)
The song "Highway Tune" (uncredited) in an episode of the television series *Shameless*.

(2017)
The song "Highway Tune" (uncredited) in an episode of the television series *Lucifer*.

(2018)
The song "Highway Tune" in the movie *Den of Thieves*.
The song "Highway Tune" in an episode of the television series *Preacher*.
The song "Safari Song" in the movie *Aquaman*.
The song "When The Curtain Falls" on the video game NHL 19.
The song "When The Curtain Falls" on the Coheed and Cambria album *The Amory Wars: Unheavenly Creatures*.

(2019)
The song "When The Curtain Falls" in an episode of the television series *Magnum P.I.*
The songs "Black Smoke Rising" and "Edge Of Darkness" in various episodes of the television series Project EVE.

MUSIC VIDEOS

(2017)
"Highway Tune," directed by Ford Fairchild.

(2018)
"When the Curtain Falls," directed by Benjamin Kutsko.

AWARDS

Loudwire Music Awards
2017-Best New Artist-won

iHeart Radio Music Awards

2019-Best Song of the Year ("Safari Song")-won
Fryderyk
2019-Best Foreign Album (*Anthem of a Peaceful Army*)-won

Grammy Awards
2019-Best New Artist-nominated. Best Rock Performance ("Highway Tune")-nominated. Best Rock Song ("Black Smoke Rising")-nominated. Best Rock Album (*From the Fires*)-won.

SOURCES

INTERVIEWS
I would like to thank Connie King, Troy Medore and Shayne Medore for their time and their memories of an all-important night in the Greta Van Fleet odyssey.

MAGAZINES
Forbes, Classic Rock, Billboard, Glide Magazine, Zebra Magazine, Newsday, The Illinois Entertainer, Rolling Stone, Blues Rock Review, Modern Drummer, Review Magazine, Scream Magazine, Drum Magazine, QRO Magazine, Music Connection, Guitar World, Screamer Magazine, Substream Magazine, Go Venue, Pittsburgh Music, Bass Player, Psychology Today, Esquire, GQ, HM Magazine

NEWSPAPERS
Huffington Post, The Advertiser, The Sydney Morning Herald, The Cleveland Scene, Detroit Metro Times, Detroit Free Press, Detroit News, Coachella Valley Weekly, Phoenix New Times, Salt Lake City Tribune, Gulf Times, Cleveland Plain Dealer, Variety, Guitar Girl, Heavy, The Associated Press, New Musical Express, Florida Times Union, Wall Street Journal, Pasadena Star News.

WEBSITES

AntiHero Magazine.com, The 405.com, The Spectrum.com, Bangs.com, Bullet Music.com, Sing Me A Song.com, Prohbtd.com, Loudsound.com, Premier Guitar.com, Columbus Calling.com, Pop Matters.com, Music Radar.com, Listen Iowa.com, Mlive.com, Fender.com, Livewire.com, Alternative Nation.com, Pollstar.com, Grown Up Rock.com, Pure Grain Audio.com, Airplay Today.com, Entertainment.com, Medleyville.us, Redburn Review.com, Setlist.com, Social Magazine.com, I'm Music.com, Sound On Sound.com, Out Of The Box.com, The Pop Breaks.com, Loudwire.com, The Red And Black.com, Mixonline.com, Metal Riot.com, Prelude Press.com, Blabbermouth.net, BTR Today.com, Decibel Geek.com, AXS.com, National Rock Review.com, Local Spins.com, Rat Rock News.com, How Was It Detroit.com, Uproxx.com, Metro Times.com, Consequence Of Sound.com, Vulture.com, Metal Sucks.com, New Jersey Arts.com, Pitchfork.com, , Kill Your Stereo.com, Metalhead Zone.com, Drum!.com, Rock Bands of LA.com

MISCELLANEOUS

KROQ radio interview, CBS San Francisco radio interview, Grammy Museum interview, Rock 95 radio interview, Greta Van Fleet twitter, Jimmy Fallon Show, Greta Van Fleet Facebook message, ABC 12. The Ladies of Comedy podcast

About the Author

New York Times bestselling author Marc Shapiro has written more than 60 nonfiction celebrity biographies, more than 24 comic books, numerous short stories and poetry, and three short-form screenplays. He is also a veteran freelance entertainment journalist.

His young adult book, *JK Rowling: The Wizard Behind Harry Potter,* was on *The New York Times* bestseller list for four straight weeks. His fact-based book *Total Titanic* was also on *The Los Angeles Times* bestseller list for four weeks. *Justin Bieber: The Fever* was on the nationwide Canadian bestseller list for several weeks.

Shapiro has written books on such personalities as Shonda Rhimes, George Harrison, Carlos Santana, Annette Funicello, Lorde, Lindsay Johan, E.L. James, Jamie Dornan, Dakota Johnson, Adele and countless others. He also co-authored the autobiography of mixed martial arts fighter Tito Ortiz, *This Is Gonna Hurt: The Life of a Mixed Martial Arts Champion.*

He is currently working on a biography of Keanu Reeves as well as updating group biographies of Beatle Wives and Beatle Kids for Riverdale Avenue Books.

Other Riverdale Avenue Books Titles by Marc Shapiro

Burn The Stage: The Rise of BTS and Korean Boy Bands

Lorde: Your Heroine, How This Young Feminist Broke the Rules and Succeeded

Legally Bieber: Justin Bieber at 18

You're Gonna Make It After All: The Life, Times and Influence of Mary Tyler Moore

Hey Joe: The Unauthorized Biography of a Rock Classic

Trump This! The Life and Times of Donald Trump, An Unauthorized Biography

The Secret Life of EL James

The Real Steele: The Unauthorized Biography of Dakota Johnson